Appliqué is a classic embroidery technique that has recently been experiencing a revival. This new book from the authors of *How to Be Creative in Textile Art* takes a fresh look at the world of appliqué and surface embellishment, showing both novices and professionals how to develop distinctive and individual designs, create exciting compositions and use unusual combinations of materials.

Moving from the historic use and cultural importance of appliqué to a range of exciting contemporary examples, the authors demonstrate the true scope, versatility and eternal relevance of appliqué techniques. They cover traditional variations – bonded appliqué, broderie Perse, cutaway appliqué and Mola work – and explain how you can push the boundaries of the traditional to create unique, personal pieces.

Full of practical advice for exploring new materials, equipment and techniques, and illustrated throughout with examples from renowned textile artists, this is the essential resource for anyone wishing to explore the cutting-edge world of appliqué.

Contemporary

Appliqué

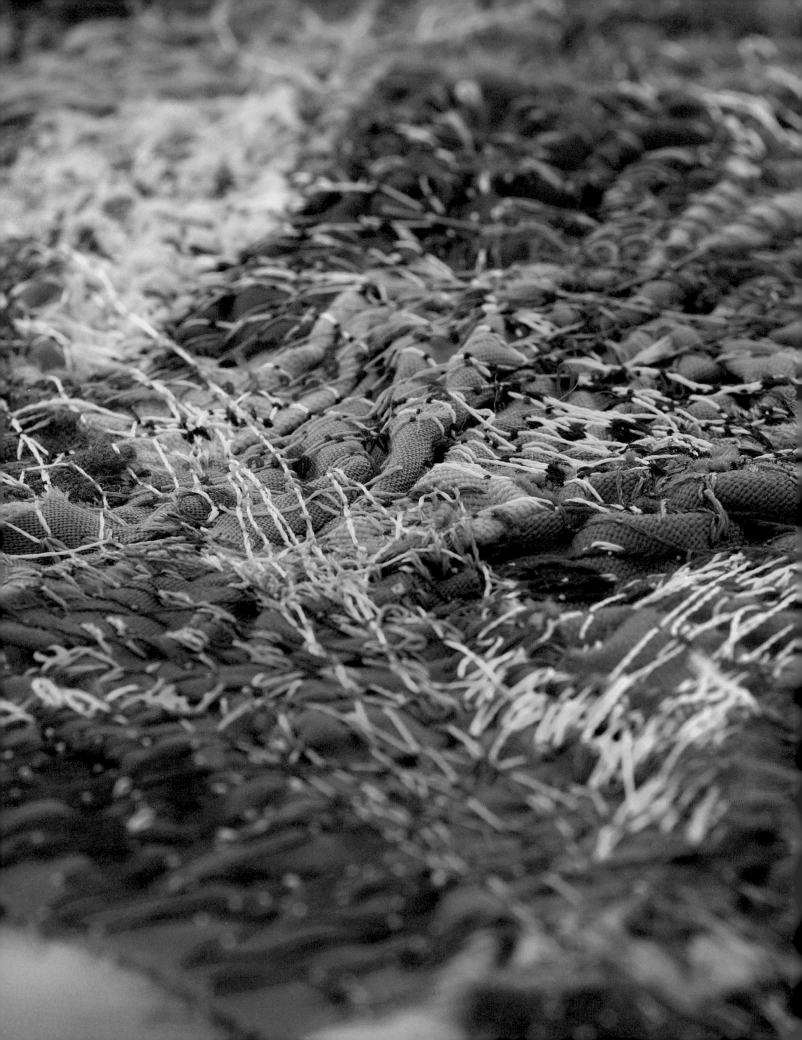

Contemporary

Appliqué

Julia Triston
Rachel Lombard

BATSFORD

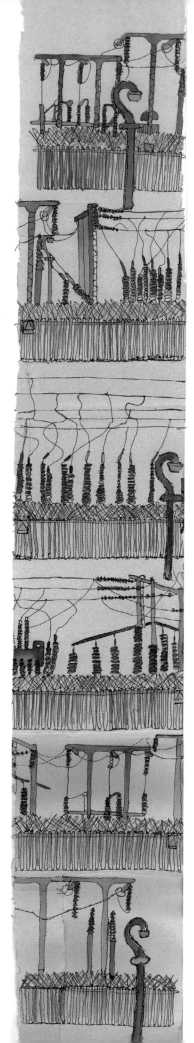

Dedication

To Zoë Triston and Tim Triston. Thanks for being such brilliant, inspiring and loving human beings; you are the best. And thanks to my mum, Joan Baker, for being there and for believing in me. To the memory of Natalie Jane Davies and 'Daisy' Jane Few Dodds: two wonderfully creative women who knew how to lead their lives to the full.
Julia Triston

Dedicated to David, with love, 'we've been a long long time together, through the hard times and the good'. To James, Christopher and Siân you are each unique and wonderful. Also to Elsie, the dog, our favourite furry friend.
Rachel Lombard

First published in the United Kingdom in 2014 by
Batsford
10 Southcombe Street
London W14 0RA
An imprint of Pavilion Books Group Ltd

ISBN: 9781849941587

A CIP catalogue record for this book is available from the British Library.

20 19 18 17 16 15 14
10 9 8 7 6 5 4 3 2 1

Printed by Craft Print Ltd, Singapore
Reproduction by Rival Colour Ltd, UK

This book can be ordered direct from the publisher at the website: www.anovabooks.com, or try your local bookshop.

Distributed in the United States and Canada by
Sterling Publishing Co.,
387 Park Avenue South, New York, NY 10016, USA

Page 1 *Sprig* (Mandy Pattullo). Hand stitched appliqué on vintage quilt fragment.

Previous page *Bright Spot* (detail) (Julia Triston). Constructed textured appliquéd surface; cotton patches applied to cotton foundation with whip stitch in free machine embroidery.

Left *Transformers* (Susan Syddall). Paper on paper appliqué with hand painting and free machine embroidery.

Contents

Foreword

This book is about appliqué – the art of decorating one fabric with another. 'Appliqué' is an umbrella term that encompasses a collection of techniques, such as layering, patching, applying and overlaying, which can be interpreted in myriad ways.

Each technical variation of appliqué has its own structure and formal method of working within set boundaries as well as the expectations of function and appearance. But these boundaries can be broken, developed and reinterpreted so that appliqué becomes contemporary and relevant for your own work and practice.

As well as setting appliqué within its historical and traditional contexts, we will take you on a journey of new ideas and imaginative ways to develop distinctive and individual designs; create exciting compositions; use unusual combinations of materials; and explore innovative and creative approaches for each method.

Enjoy discovering the exciting possibilities of appliqué!

Below *Tea Time Treats* (Donna Cheshire). From left to right: 'Rosie Lea', 'Garden Party', 'It's Always Sunny in the Tea Tent'; collaged appliquéd surfaces with free machine embroidery on recycled tins.

Right *Flourish* (detail) (Emily Notman). Bonded, stitched and burned appliquéd surface with natural and handmade embellishments.

Introduction

The possibilities for the exploration of appliqué are endless. It can be explored two- and three-dimensionally; it can be delicate and transparent or thick and chunky; it can be on a large or more intimate scale; it can be created in fabrics, plastics, papers or metals; it can be used in layers and multiples to repeat patterns; it can play with shape and form; and it can be the main feature or a smaller component or highlight of a piece of work.

In its simplest form, appliqué is the technique of stitching a small patch of cloth on to the surface of a larger foundation cloth, and was traditionally used to repair small holes and tears in clothing and furnishings.

From these utilitarian beginnings, appliqué has evolved to become an expressive and creative art form in its own right. In contemporary appliqué, the emphasis is now on surface embellishment and decoration. Wide ranges of colours, textures and materials can be innovatively combined to create individual and personal textile artwork, from quilts and soft furnishings to clothing, jewellery and wall art.

In this book we will build on a foundation of traditional knowledge and skills, and show you that appliqué is very much alive. It is relevant to, and at the cutting edge of, contemporary surface decoration and textile design.

Part 1

Appliqué
in context

Historical perspectives

Ancient appliqué

Medieval appliqué

Sixteenth to eighteenth
    centuries

Nineteenth and twentieth
    century to the present day

Cultural contexts

Dress

Banners

Narrative hangings

Interiors

Symbolism – shape
    and colour

Appliqué now

Planning and forming ideas

What shall I make?

Keeping records

Conclusion to Part 1

Historical perspectives

Historically, textiles were highly prized and valued for their beauty as well as their function, as they were time-consuming and labour-intensive to produce. Because there were few alternative materials suitable for wrapping, carrying, sheltering, shrouding and clothing, textiles held a status and importance in everybody's lives; we have lost this respect for textiles today. In our modern throwaway world we take for granted the availability, variety and cost of textiles.

Appliqué has existed for thousands of years. Although textiles by their nature deteriorate and disintegrate over time and colours fade, beautiful examples of exquisitely designed and intricately worked appliqué have survived from all over the world. These give us a tantalizing insight into the historic use and importance of appliqué, and an appreciation of the technical skill and creativity of the people who used this method of decorating one cloth with another.

Ancient appliqué

Archaeological excavations reveal that richly decorated appliquéd and embroidered textiles were closely associated with, and reflected the elite status of, the deceased. They were entombed with the revered dead to accompany them to the afterlife, giving us a fascinating insight into the everyday lives and lost worlds of ancient civilizations.

Some of the earliest surviving appliqués have been discovered in Ancient Egyptian tombs. Mummified animals have been found wrapped in appliquéd cloths, and a linen collar with appliquéd petals dating back 3,000 years was discovered in Tutankhamen's tomb.

In southern Siberian tombs, examples of felt and leather appliqué, dating back to the fifth century BC, were discovered in the 1920s. These highly decorative and incredibly well-preserved appliquéd carpets and wall hangings, saddle blankets and coverings were made by the early nomadic tribes of the Pazyryk region of the Altai Mountains. It is astonishing that these beautiful textiles really are 5,000 years old – the colours, textures, designs and workmanship are so intact that they could have been made yesterday. It is only because of exceptional climatic conditions that these precious ancient textiles have survived.

Although much of the physical evidence of appliqué has been lost with the passage of time through deterioration, wear and tear, and recycling, there is such a consistency in the use of materials, designs and technique, it is obvious that the traditions of appliqué have been passed from generation to generation through the ages.

For centuries, textiles were a valuable trading commodity and, as they were traded between cultures, ideas about appliqué were exchanged, designs were reinterpreted and techniques were adapted to make them more suitable for use with locally available materials and cultural tastes.

Previous page
Antique Hmong Tribe traditional costume fragment (detail), (collection of Julia Triston). Hand-appliquéd cottons onto fabric strips with embroidered surface decoration.

Right Saddlecloth, 218 x 68cm (86 x 27in), 5th–4th century BC (Pazyryk culture, Siberia, collection of The State Hermitage Museum, St Petersburg). The whole surface of this white felt saddlecloth, except for a narrow band beneath the saddle, is covered with ornamental inlay felt appliqué, with horseshoe shapes in the border.

Medieval appliqué

Disease also played its part in the development of appliqué. In England, the Black Death of 1348 contributed to the destruction of the system of medieval guilds and workshops where skilled textile workers and embroiderers produced vestments and hangings for the Church and the wealthy elite. The style of embroidery at this time, known as *Opus Anglicanum* (English work), predominantly involved exquisite metal thread and silk stitching, and was intricate, expensive and time-consuming to produce. These pieces were highly valued and exported throughout Europe.

The decimation of a highly skilled professional workforce had a dramatic impact on the way that textiles were decorated: appliqué increasingly began to be used as a less costly substitute for solid embroidery on military regalia and ecclesiastical vestments, and European embroidery became more of a domestic art form. Appliqué was widely used to suit the needs and resources of the household and continued to be popular as it could involve the endless recycling and reworking of older textiles. It was used on covers, household linen, curtains, clothing and furnishings as a decorative feature and for small-scale mending.

Sixteenth to eighteenth centuries

In large, grand households, where a greater wealth of resources was available, appliqué featured on a more significant scale. The important allegorical Hardwick Hall panels, stitched by Bess of Hardwick, Countess of Shrewsbury, are a fine example of sixteenth-century appliqué. They show the use of recycled vestments, which would have found their way into private hands at the time of the Reformation.

Left Embroidery for a casket *c.*1650 depicting King Solomon and the Queen of Sheba (collection of The Bowes Museum, Barnard Castle). Raised embroidery in coloured silks and metal threads with needle lace and seed pearls, applied as wired, padded slips to a silk foundation later (probably in the 1960s) mounted over a wooden carcass.

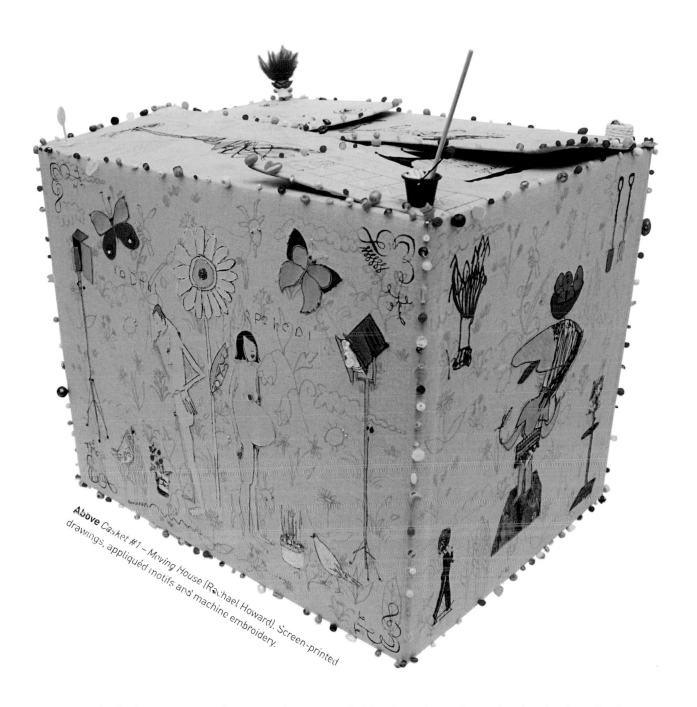

Above *Casket #1 – Moving House (Rachael Howard). Screen-printed drawings, appliquéd motifs and machine embroidery.*

In the late seventeenth century there was a fashion for a three-dimensional style of appliqué known as raised work or stumpwork. This lively, secular form of English embroidery adorned caskets, mirrors and narrative pictures, often of a biblical theme. Individual motifs were stitched and then padded and applied as a 'slip' to a background of silk, satin or velvet.

An important step in the history of appliqué was the development of a patched and pieced style of quilt-making by settlers in North America throughout the seventeenth century. Trade restrictions put in place by the British severely limited the import of cloth into North America, which forced the settlers to find ever more inventive and creative ways to use and reuse available fabrics. By the time the British lifted the trading restrictions in 1826, the integration of appliqué into quilt-making was firmly established and continues to develop to this day. Fine examples are the album quilts of the mid-nineteenth century and the distinctive Baltimore quilts, many of which were stitched by groups of women working together.

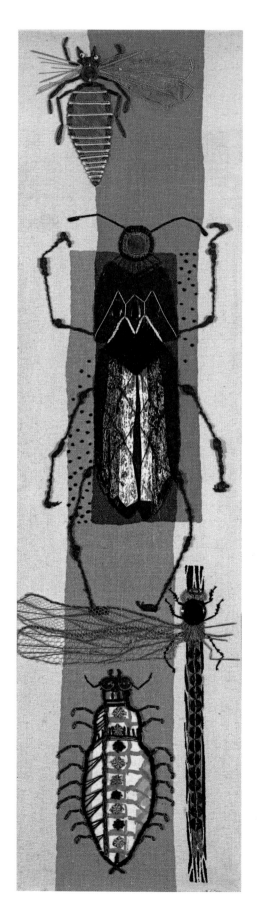

Nineteenth and twentieth century to the present day

Technology has also played its part in the development of appliqué. With the introduction of aniline dyes in the 1850s, fabrics could be mass-produced in more vivid colours, which appealed to an increasingly insatiable market for domestic needlework goods.

Victorian Britain developed a passion for these newly discovered lurid colours and enthusiastically incorporated them into fancy needlework projects, reflecting the Victorian appetite for highly decorative and ornate surfaces. Their love of busy surfaces was translated into the technique of crazy patchwork – an appliqué style created from an assortment of colours, textures and irregular shapes, which were randomly pieced together in the making process, then further embellished with decorative hand embroidery.

As a reaction to this overwhelming riot of colour and pattern, Jessie Newbury and Ann Macbeth (notable teachers of artistic needlework at Glasgow School of Art) championed the ethics of the Arts and Crafts Movement led by William Morris and his contemporaries. At the heart of the movement was a belief in the revival of traditional craft skills and the rejection of the industrialization of production. For the first time the relationship between materials, technique, working process and aesthetic form was considered. Appliqués were designed with simple, clean lines and harmonious colour palettes.

Left *Insects*, 1928 (Margaret Nicholson, collection of Anthea Godfrey). Hand appliqué and embroidery onto printed ground.

Right *Pawnbroker Crazy Coverlet*, 1877 (collection of Quilt Museum and Gallery, York). Recycled velvets and silks; applied and elaborately decorated with embroidery embellishment. Purchased from a pawnbrokers in London in the 1920s/30s after the death of the owner.

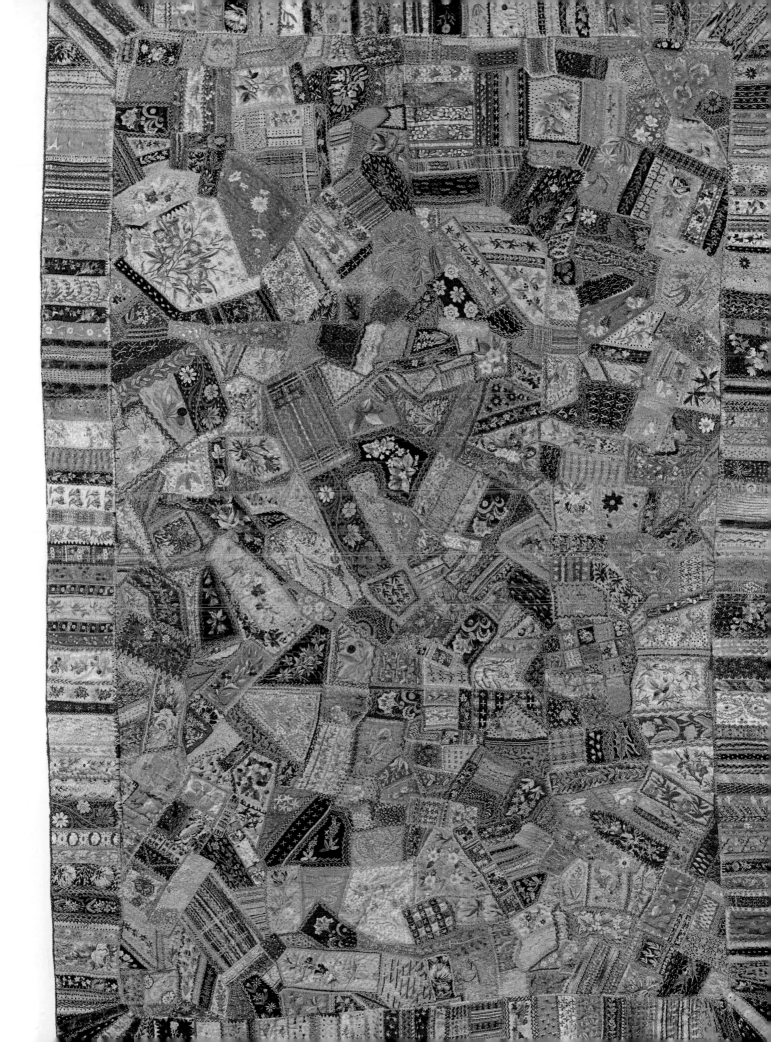

Throughout the twentieth century, appliqué continued to be used in more diverse and experimental ways as an art form in its own right. Rebecca Crompton was an influential embroiderer and teacher who emphasized the importance of design rather than the perfection of stitch technique. Her appliqués of the 1930s show a contemporary approach to design combined with a new and exciting use of the sewing machine as a drawing tool.

Constance Howard, an important and deeply influential figure in twentieth-century embroidery and a pioneer in textile art, pushed the boundaries of appliqué and continued to assert the significance of textile art as a vehicle for artistic self-expression.

Above *The Magic Garden*, 1937 (Rebecca Crompton, collection of Victoria & Albert Museum). Plain and patterned fabrics appliquéd by hand and further embellished with textured surface stitching.

Right *Two Doves*, 1950 (Constance Howard, collection of Embroiderers' Guild). Applied stylized imagery onto silk ground with hand embroidery.

Above *Overlord Embroidery* (detail), 240cm x 90cm (95 x 35in), (collection of D-Day Museum, Portsmouth). This is the fourteenth panel of thirty-four, recording events of 6th June 1944; all panels are worked to the same size and hand stitched in cotton and linen.

The world of fashion offers more opportunities – each garment has the potential to be a blank canvas for appliqué. Throughout the twentieth century, appliqué increasingly featured in fashion, often taking inspiration from artists of the day, as in the case of fashion designer Elsa Schiaparelli, who had close links with Salvador Dalí and the Surrealists. Her appliqué designs are distinctive and still look quirky and contemporary today.

Other notable art movements have also influenced surface decoration in fashion and textiles: these include the Cubists with their abstract concepts; the Dadaists with their use of found materials and collage/mixed-media compositions; and the proponents of Op Art, who created the illusion of movement across a surface. Naturally, artists respond to the economic, political, intellectual and emotional events facing them, and constantly view, review and use their materials accordingly. New ideas and methods emerge, and in turn directly translate and revolutionize the way textile artists interact and respond to materials.

Appliqué has also been used to document, celebrate and commemorate important historical and social events. An excellent example of an appliqué document is the *Overlord Embroidery*, which records the D-Day invasion of Normandy by Allied forces on 6 June 1944. This magnificent narrative appliqué of 34 panels, each 240 x 90cm (95 x 35in), was designed by Sandra Lawrence and took embroiderers at the Royal School of Needlework five years to complete.

Beryl Dean's 1977 *Jubilee Cope* for the Bishop of London depicts St Paul's Cathedral and many of London's spectacular churches. The collaged appliqué design expresses the sense of unity between Church and State that was celebrated at Queen Elizabeth II's Silver Jubilee.

In the 1980s, Tracey Emin, one of the Young British Artists, became renowned for her shocking autobiographical artwork, much of which featured appliqué. Her pieces (made from recycled materials that held emotional significance for her) referenced intimate, personal experiences and frequently challenged the viewer.

The attitude towards, and the application of, appliqué techniques have changed over time. Appliqué has grown away from its original practical purpose of reusing materials for patching and mending – this adaptable technique is continually developing, expanding and being reinterpreted to suit contemporary tastes, trends and styles.

Today, many textile artists incorporate appliqué freely and spontaneously in their work, celebrating the fact that it is now firmly embedded in the language of art, textiles and stitch.

Left *Autumn Sunset* (Julie Bull). Hand appliquéd illustration with dyed and recycled fabrics, from 'Tales from the Welsh Wood' series.

Right *Chimney Pots* (Laura McCafferty). Screen-printed and hand-appliquéd composition with re-purposed fabrics.

Cultural contexts

Textiles are part of everyday life in all cultures. From clothing and bags to bedding, seat covers and shelters – we live with them and appreciate them, but can use them unthinkingly. In contrast, our attitude towards textiles that have a special context and bear a significance in our lives – for example a wedding dress, a trade-union banner or military colours – have an intrinsic emotional meaning and value invested in them. Through them we can proudly express our cultural, ethnic, religious and political identities.

Throughout the world, many indigenous communities have developed their own distinctive styles of appliqué, often using locally sourced raw materials such as felt from animal hair, fabrics from processed plant materials, or leathers and silks from animals. Together with their stylized designs, these types of appliqué – such as mola work by the Kuna Indians of Central America, leather appliqué from Hungary and characteristic appliqués from the tribal people of south east Asia – have become synonymous with their cultural identities.

Appliqué, in its many guises, is used worldwide as surface decoration and has played an important role in the adornment of culturally significant textiles.

Above *Roundels*, Meo Tribe costume fragments (collection of Julia Triston). These individually styled antique appliqué roundels are used as an embellishment on the sleeves and front panels of the traditional black tunics worn by men and women.

Left Antique Hmong Tribe costume fragment (detail) (collection of Julia Triston). Hand-appliquéd strips worked onto printed cotton and silks with surface embroidery. The appliquéd fabrics that have worn away have left a tracery of tiny hand stitches.

Below Decorative costume strip, Lisu Hill Tribe, Thailand (collection of Julia Triston). This vibrant, modern-day stripy band is constructed from lengths of coloured cotton fabrics with folded square inserts to create the triangles and central divided squares. Machine stitched onto gauze foundation.

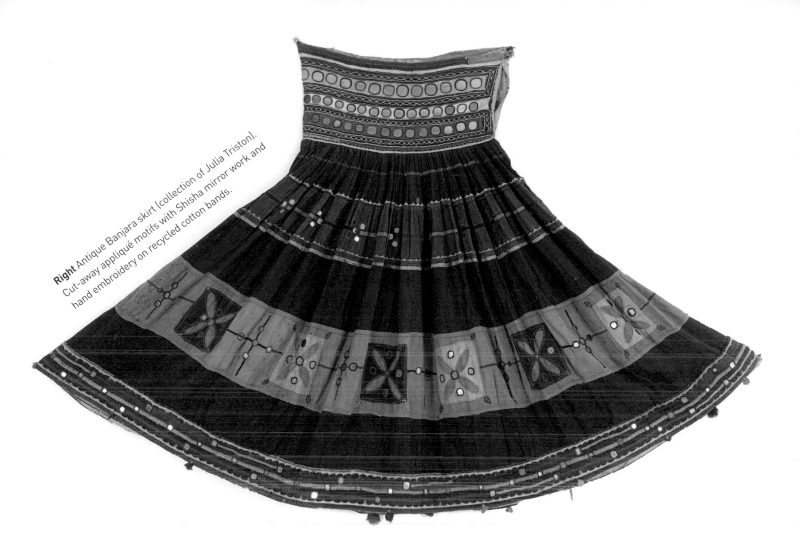

Dress

Dress can signify membership of a club, group, class, tribe, nation or culture; intentionally or unintentionally it visually denotes, displays and expresses an identity. Internationally, appliqué features on and decorates national costumes, ecclesiastical dress, military regalia and civilian uniforms.

Whether it is an appliquéd grosgrain ribbon on a uniform, a patterned border on a skirt, or a collection of badges on a biker's jacket, appliqué can distinguish membership of a group, rank, status and gender and delineate a particular role or level of achievement and responsibility.

The Kuba people of the Congo are noted for their strong, abstract appliqué designs on ceremonial skirts and aprons. Made from patched panels of woven raffia palm leaves, these are very stiff and so have to be washed and pounded before they can be worn. The holes that appear as a consequence are covered with decorative appliqué.

Left Drawing of ceremonial Kuba skirt (Julia Triston). Koh-i-noor paints on khadi paper, showing traditional shapes and patterns.

Banners

Appliqué is one of the most popular ways of decorating a background fabric to make a banner. Banners may convey a visually succinct message through the use of a logo, a motto, or particular colours associated with a group, society, movement, political party or a union. Appliqué is particularly suitable because it's a relatively easy and quick technique to use, it can be bright and bold, and it suits designs of all shapes and sizes.

Sometimes banners are made with lots of consideration given to the design and detail, and are unique and beautiful works of art. At other times they are made in a hurry with passion and determination, with materials found around the house, as an immediate response to rapidly unfolding political events.

At meetings, conventions, stalls, protest marches, gatherings and parades people show their allegiance to ideas and identities by carrying and congregating around banners. Banners can become a permanent and historical record of both local and global social and political movements.

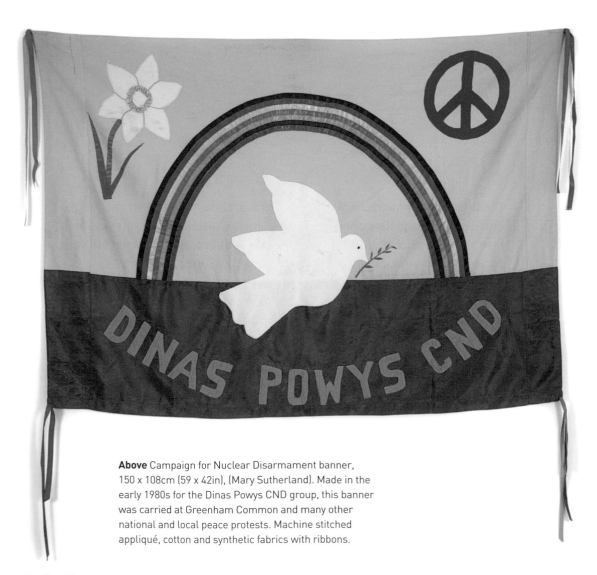

Above Campaign for Nuclear Disarmament banner, 150 x 108cm (59 x 42in), (Mary Sutherland). Made in the early 1980s for the Dinas Powys CND group, this banner was carried at Greenham Common and many other national and local peace protests. Machine stitched appliqué, cotton and synthetic fabrics with ribbons.

Narrative hangings

Appliqué has been used across nations and cultures to record historical events visually, tell a story, convey a moral message and spread information.

For example, a decorative appliqué hanging known as an arpillera is a three-dimensional hand-sewn textile picture, which originated in Chile during the Pinochet regime. Female political prisoners began making arpilleras and used them as a way of smuggling notes to the outside world. The guards saw the arpilleras as inconsequential 'women's work', and did not search them for hidden messages.

Today these distinct, colourful works of art depict everyday scenes, stories of country life, farming, weddings and fiestas, and are made by women in co-operatives, many of whom have been displaced from their traditional mountain lives. The sale of arpilleras has become an important source of income for many families, enabling them to improve their standard of living and educate their children.

The Fon people of Benin have a long tradition of appliquéing cloth and are still renowned for their narrative wall hangings today. Designed and stitched by artists, these appliquéd cloths depict scenes of daily life and have been used to describe historical events. Each appliquéd image or symbol represents a particular sound or word; when the whole cloth is 'read', an overall picture of an event or story is told. Traditionally, friends gathering at a funeral would appliqué a cloth to record and celebrate their loved one's life and achievements.

India is well known for its colourful and expressive embroidery and appliqué work, which plays an important part in everyday life and ceremonial occasions. Narrative cloths are used everywhere in India, in the form of torans, sankias, dharaniyos and chaklas: richly stitched and appliquéd bold, bright and beautiful styles of wall hangings. These textiles are symbolic, containing cultural and religious imagery such as the Tree of Life, elephants and peacocks, and are used as a talisman to ward off evil spirits and to bring luck to the household.

Above Arab Spring appliqué quilt, 216 x 200cm (85 x 79in), (Hany Abdul Kader, collection of the Oriental Museum, Durham University). A contemporary account, made in secret, that records and depicts the events in Tahrir Square during the demonstrations and protests of the Egyptian Arab Spring Revolution 2011.

Interiors

People have always had a desire to beautify and personalize their surroundings and belongings. Because appliqué is such a versatile technique, it is not surprising that it frequently adorns textile surfaces, at a large and small scale, in both public and private spaces.

Left Khayamiya hanging, 150 x 150cm (59 X 59in), (Tarek Fattoh, collection of Rachel Lombard). Egyptian cottons in cream, blue and turquoise, hand stitched in a pattern of overlapping rings and lotus flowers.

Large scale

Khayamiya is a style of decorative appliqué, traditionally used to form and decorate the interiors of tents throughout the Arab world. These intricate, large-scale hangings continue to be made by the tent-makers of Cairo – professional male artists – who can spend months designing and working on one appliqué. Popular designs include calligraphic text, ancient Egyptian imagery and geometric, arabesque patterns.

Appliqué has frequently been a favoured technique for the decoration of church altar cloths and frontals. Traditionally designed by a professional artist or broderer, and stitched by women from the church community, these large-scale cloths are decorated with symbols and colours that represent particular times in the Christian calendar. Designs are carefully considered and have to be approved by church authorities; from conception to realization and installation, they can take years to complete.

Above Lenten altar frontal on high altar, Durham Cathedral (designed by Tracy A Franklin). Appliquéd silk and leather onto a linen ground, hand stitched by Durham Cathedral Broderers.

Below Lenten altar frontal, crown of thorns and desert grasses (detail), Durham Cathedral. Close up of appliqué work in progress.

Small scale

From cushions and lampshades to towels and tea cosies, appliqué adorns a huge variety of small-scale domestic items. Small appliquéd motifs can add a tiny detail and focus, whereas larger appliquéd motifs can almost completely cover and dominate a background, forming the whole design.

Right *Play With Me* (Tilleke Schwarz). Hand embroidery on linen with small applied motifs, based on imagery and text encountered in everyday life (see detail on page 73).

Below Cushion collection inspired by the life of Dorothy Wordsworth (Poppy Dinsdale). Polychromatic prints with 'feature' appliqué patches.

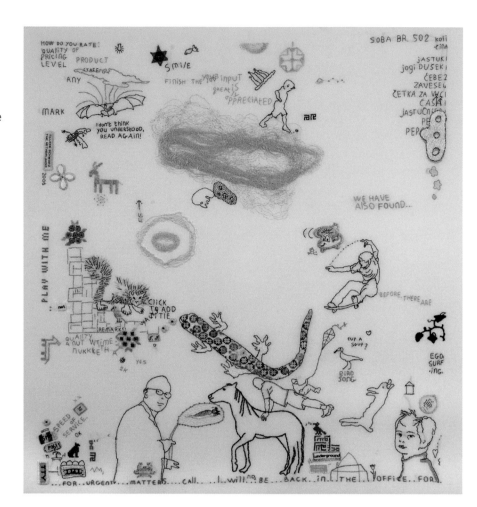

Symbolism – shape and colour

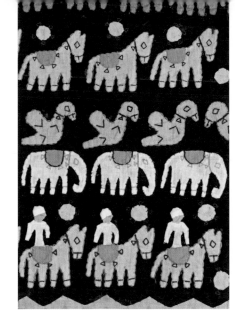

Animals, mythological beasts, geometric and floral patterns and the human form are the most commonly found motifs in appliqué work. They are often simplified and stylized to become symbolic rather than representational. Many designs hold meanings that can be understood internationally – for example a circle to symbolize the sun. Other widely recognizable stylized designs include the Tree of Life and religious imagery such as crosses, stars, eyes, fish and spirals.

The symbolism of colour is both fascinating and complex. Colour is used across all cultures to express national identity, team allegiance and close associations with folklore. It can also be used to define gender, indicate political affiliation and mark festivals and religious ceremonies.

Above and below Indian folk art wall hanging (collection of Julia Triston). Simplified and stylized motifs hand appliquéd and roughly outlined in hand embroidery.

In the worldwide market, appliquéd textiles go in and out of fashion, but in cultures with a strong textile tradition they remain part of everyday experience.

The age of information we live in has enabled many of us to access a wider global marketplace, both via the Internet and by travel. As a consequence, we have developed a deeper understanding and appreciation of the variety and quality of appliqué art, and an ability to set it within its wider cultural context.

Whether folk art or fine art, appliqué remains a vital and lively expression of tradition and culture.

Appliqué now

Contemporary appliqué is a diverse, exciting and expressive art form. Textile artists, quilters, fashion and costume designers, interior designers and toymakers are increasingly using appliqué in inventive ways. Appliqué is also creeping into the work of fine artists, jewellery makers and installation artists. The boundaries and traditions of appliqué are constantly being pushed, challenged and redefined.

In appliqué today, almost anything goes. Sometimes defined as layering, collage or mixed-media work, and sometimes used unknowingly as a technique, appliqué is a versatile and creative medium using a wide range of materials.

The Internet allows appliqué work to be seen, exhibited, bought and sold with ease. Ideas and techniques can be demonstrated, exchanged and discussed. This sharing of information is inspiring and can enrich your own design and stitch work.

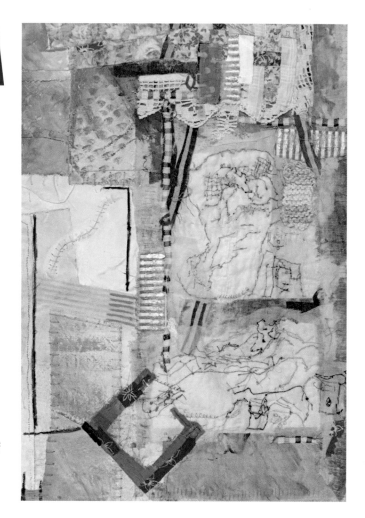

Above *Drifting Away III* (detail) (Jae Maries). Contemporary mixed-media, wall-hung textile documenting the gentle confinement of a nursing home; materials include calico, oil paint, paper and recycled fabrics with hand and machine embroidery.

Planning and forming ideas

When planning your own appliqué projects, there are important questions to ask yourself:

• What do I want to make?
• What is my budget?
• What is my timescale?
• Will the finished project be functional, decorative, or both?
• Will it be worn?
• Will it be double-sided or reversible?
• Will it be regularly handled or used? If so, by whom?
• Will it need to be washed?
• Will it be on display? If so, where and how?
• Will it need to be transported or stored? If so, how and where?

These questions will enable you to define what you are going to make and to consider the practicalities involved. It is useful to set parameters and this will lead to a more creative and successful outcome.

Above & *Holi: Indian Spring* (Julia Triston). Painted
and block-printed papers and silk fragments
collaged to linen with cellulose paste, free
machine embroidery and hand stitch.

What shall I make?

Appliqué projects can be small or large in scale, straightforward or complicated, plain or intricate, a small detail or an overall design, two-dimensional or three-dimensional ... the possibilities are endless! You could decorate a ready-made item or surface with appliqué (for example, a book cover or a jacket lapel), or you could construct a whole piece from scratch (such as a needle case or a soft toy) and include appliqué as an integral part of the design and making process.

How you finish your work will depend on what it is and how it will be used. If it is an item that will be handled every day and washed a lot, all edges and motifs should be thoroughly stitched and secured. If it is a piece to display, edges can be left unfinished and stitches can be less robust.

Above *Pottering in the Garden Number 1: Sunshine Days* (Donna Cheshire).

Below *Button Necklace* (Lizzie Searle).

Accessories	Bags	Handbag • Shopping bag • Evening bag • Clutch • Holdall • Sports kit bag • Laundry bag • Make-up bag • Sponge bag • Shoe bag • Peg bag
	Cases	Pencil case • Needle case • Mobile-phone cover • Tablet computer cover • Glasses case • Wallet or purse • Pyjama case • Hot-water bottle cover
	Wearables	Scarf or bandana • Gloves • Hat • Cap Fascinator • Jewellery • Badge • Belt
Interiors	Cushions	Ring cushion • Bolster • Floor cushion • Chair cushion • Pincushion

	Household linen	Tablecloth • Table runner • Table mat • Napkin • Tea towel • Towel • Tea cosy • Egg cosy • Apron • Bedspread • Pillowcase • Blanket • Throw • Quilt • Blinds • Curtains
	Miscellaneous	Lampshade • Book cover • Photo frame • Ornament • Sculpture • Box • Map
Babies and children	Playthings	Doll • Soft toy • Puppet • Cloth book • Play mat • Mobile
Decorative display	Hangings	Bunting • Banners • Flags • Wall art • Framed picture • Wall hanging • Panel • Christmas decorations • Signs
Apparel	Fashion	Top • Knitwear • Skirt • Trousers • Jacket or coat • Shawl or wrap • Dressing gown • Lingerie • Fancy dress costume • Footwear
	Clothing details	Hem • Border • Cuff • Collar • Lapel • Pocket

It can be both exciting and daunting to start a project. Taking the time carefully to consider what you are going to make, how you are going to make it and reflect on what you want to achieve, is time well spent. This process will ensure that your project is manageable in terms of time, costs, materials, personal energy and ability.

Planning a project and forming your ideas should be fun and enjoyable. There are no boundaries or constraints: the possibilities for contemporary appliqué can be as free as your imagination.

Above *Wedding Bag* (Rachel Lombard). Frayed silk appliquéd banner of machine-stitched words on a hand-stitched and embellished silk ground.

Left *Little People* (Tania Sneesby). Brooches made from painted cotton and free-machined appliqué.

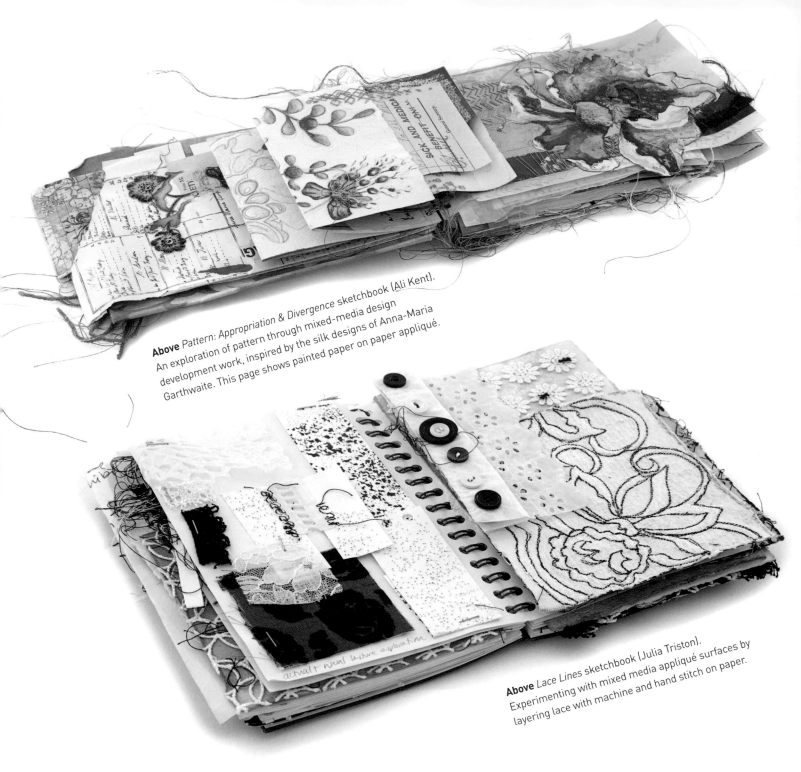

Above *Pattern: Appropriation & Divergence* sketchbook (Ali Kent). An exploration of pattern through mixed-media design development work, inspired by the silk designs of Anna-Maria Garthwaite. This page shows painted paper on paper appliqué.

Above *Lace Lines* sketchbook (Julia Triston). Experimenting with mixed media appliqué surfaces by layering lace with machine and hand stitch on paper.

Keeping records

There are many ways of recording your making process – you could create a pinboard of ideas, keep a journal, take photographs of your progress or write a blog – but we recommend keeping a sketchbook. A sketchbook gives you the opportunity to collect together your ideas, thoughts, plans, possibilities, samples, design-development work, swatches, notes and annotations in one place. Keeping an honest, ongoing account of your progression is an extremely useful way of analysing and evaluating how your ideas have evolved, advanced and been refined. There is no right or wrong way to keep a sketchbook but each one can become a valuable and inspiring resource recording your personal journey. You don't have to share this with anyone – it can be entirely private (see Further Reading, page 126).

Conclusion to Part 1

As we have seen, appliqué is an ancient, international way of decorating cloth, which can have a deep cultural significance. Yet it is a technique that is at the forefront of contemporary art textiles. In Part 2 we will consider the importance of design skills for appliqué and examine the essential elements for a successful design.

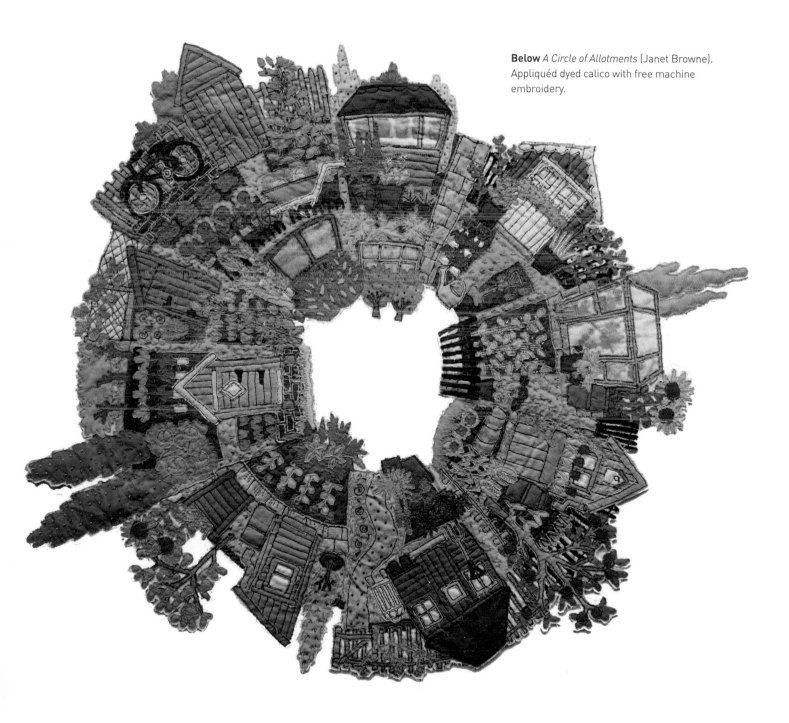

Below *A Circle of Allotments* (Janet Browne). Appliquéd dyed calico with free machine embroidery.

Design skills

Design for appliqué

Why design?

In this chapter we lay out a framework that will enable you to identify, analyse and apply the elements and principles of design that should be taken into consideration when designing an appliqué project.

Individual elements can be studied and explored in isolation, but the most successful composition will consider them collectively and in relation to each other.

An appreciation of the elements and principles of design will enable you to develop a visual language so that you can truly understand and critically evaluate what works within a piece of artwork, and what doesn't (and why).

Formal elements

The formal elements of design are the components or building blocks used to create a successful visual composition: these are the essential foundations of good design. The five main formal elements of design are:

• Colour
• Line
• Shape
• Form
• Texture

Above *Artifact* (Dorothy Caldwell). Wax and silkscreen resist on black cotton, discharged, hand stitching and appliqué.

Previous page *Colour Study* (detail) (Julia Triston). Fragments of cottons and silks appliquéd to felt with an embellishing machine then decorated with buttons and hand embroidery.

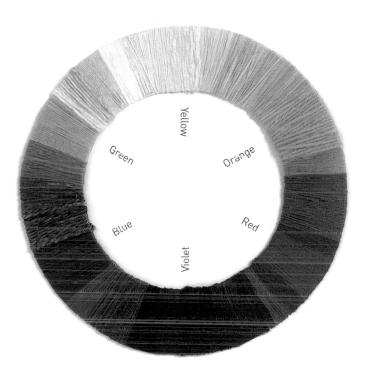

Colour

Everybody recognizes what colour is, and we all choose and use it in our everyday lives. Colour has the strongest visual impact of all the formal elements and can express a mood, an atmosphere, an emotion, depth and the illusion of space. Colour can be defined in terms of:

- **Primary colours** Yellow, red and blue
- **Secondary colours** Made by mixing the primary colours to make orange, violet and green
- **Tertiary colours** Made by mixing a primary colour with one of its secondaries: yellow-orange, red-orange, red-violet, blue-violet, blue-green and yellow-green
- **Complementary colours** These are opposites on the colour wheel and produce the most intense contrasts when used together – yellow and violet, red and green, and blue and orange
- **Analogous colours** Three colours that sit side by side on the colour wheel; when used together, they form a harmonious colour scheme
- **Value** The relative lightness or darkness of a colour; can be varied by adding white to create a tint, or adding black to create a shade
- **Saturation** The depth of brightness or dullness in an individual colour
- **Temperature** The 'feel' of a colour or combination of colours – hot/warm (reds, oranges, yellows) and cold/cool (violets, blues, greens)

Above left Colour wheel (Catherine Gowthorpe). Thread wrappings to demonstrate primary, secondary and tertiary colours.

Above *Summer Heat* (detail) (Ruth Issett). Hand-dyed fabrics using Procion MX, layered and hand stitched.

Line

Line is one-dimensional; it has a beginning and an end and joins two points together in a continuous movement across a surface. It has length and direction, can express a mood or an emotion and can create an illusion. Lines are used to form and define boundaries and emphasize edges. Lines can be distinguished as follows:

- **Quality** The way a line looks (for example, faint, contrasting, heavy, thick, bold, fading).
- **Direction** The way a line moves (for example, horizontally, vertically, diagonally; it can meander, radiate, spiral, curve or zigzag).
- **Implied** Marks that hint at a line (a row of dots, a series of dashes or carefully aligned shapes) arranged so that our brains fill in the gaps to complete the picture.

Right From the top: implied lines; straight lines; curved lines; angular lines; crossed lines (drawings by Julia Triston).

Below *Illumination* (Rachel Lombard). Dyed cotton-wool paper background with applied machine-stitched thread and snipped fabric curls, surrounded by lines of twisted chain stitch.

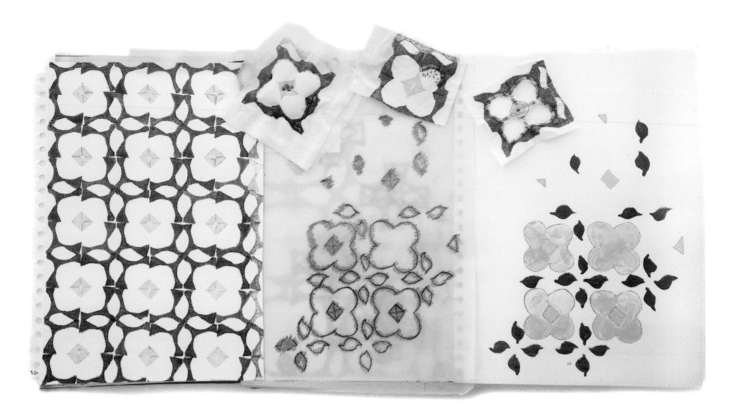

Shape

A shape is an area enclosed by lines or trapped by boundaries. It is two-dimensional and self-contained. It is flat and can be defined by its width, height and area, but not its depth. It can have a distinct outline, or a visually perceived edge created by a contrasting area of colour or texture surrounding it. Shape can be considered in terms of being:

- **Geometric** These shapes can be simple mathematical shapes drawn with a ruler or compass (such as a circle, square or triangle) or complex designs of repeated patterns worked out on graph paper (such as arabesque or strapwork tessellations).

- **Organic** These shapes are usually drawn freehand and take their inspiration from natural forms; they have softer, curvy edges, such as flowing botanical shapes and free-form asymmetrical motifs.

- **Positive or negative** A design placed on a background is referred to as the 'positive'; this creates an area around it which becomes the 'negative' space, and good design considers both equally.

- **Abstracted** An abstracted shape is the simplification of a complex object or design, which is pared down to its basic outlines and becomes representational and stylized rather than realistic.

- **Distorted** This is the disproportionate highlighting of one single aspect of a shape to emphasize a point, meaning or feature, such as the first letter in a word, lips on a face, or the length of legs on an animal to indicate its speed.

Top Appliqué panel sketchbook (Caroline Whitehead). Design work showing repeat motifs and pattern development with trial stitch samples.

Above Cushion with feature appliqué panel (Caroline Whitehead). Block-printed cotton with hand embroidery, machine stitch and embellishments, applied as a panel for a decorative cushion cover.

Form

A form is a three-dimensional object which has a height, width and depth. It can be hollow or solid; it has an outside and an inside and can be viewed in the round. Weight, mass and volume are also important properties of this formal element. Form can be analysed in term of its:

- **Materials** These can be manipulated, sculpted, moulded, padded and constructed.
- **Function** It can be wearable, sculptural, ornamental, practical or interactive.
- **Structure** This could be light and airy, dense and compacted, or flexible and malleable.
- **Scale** This can be large or small, proportionate or disproportionate, surprising or challenging.

Above Three-dimensional paper forms (Rachel Lombard). Experimenting with the potential of form with painted-paper cones.

Right *Jennifer* (Joanne Edwards). Three-dimensional jewellery created with manipulated and layered felt forms.

Right Texture sample (detail) (Julia Triston). Assorted neutral fabrics have been stuffed, gathered, plaited, rolled, twisted, woven, frayed, burned, ruched and knotted, then applied to a foundation fabric to create a densely textured surface.

Texture

Texture is about the quality of a surface. It can be described as either actual/tactile, which is the physical sensation of touching a surface, or visual/implied, which is the illusion of a surface portrayed as it feels (for example a photograph of a crumbling stone wall looks rough but in reality feels smooth). The appearance of a textured surface changes with light. A strong bright light creates shadows that accentuate raised areas, giving an illusion of depth, whereas a softer light will reduce textural contrasts. Texture can be described in terms of the qualities below:

- **Hard** A rigid, solid surface that has no 'give' (such as Formica, ceramic tiles, metal).
- **Soft** A pliable, squishy surface that 'gives' to the touch (such as foam sheets, alpaca wool, velvet).
- **Rough** An uneven, irregular surface (such as coir matting, tree bark, stones).
- **Smooth** An even, regular surface (such as polished marble, shiny paper, holly leaves).
- **Shiny** A reflective, glossy surface (such as mother-of-pearl, mirror glass, glazed pottery).
- **Matt** A non-reflective, lustreless surface (such as plaster, denim, glass worn smooth by the sea).

By understanding and analysing the formal elements of design, you will be able to use them purposefully to achieve the outcome you want.

Formal principles

The formal principles of design must be applied when arranging and organizing the design elements, in order to realize an aesthetically accomplished composition. The five main principles are:

- Balance
- Scale and proportion
- Emphasis and contrast
- Rhythm and repetition
- Unity and harmony

Balance

In a two-dimensional context, balance is the distribution and careful arrangement of formal design elements to create a visual equilibrium around a horizontal, vertical or diagonal axis.

The balance of a design can be described as symmetrical or formal when two halves of the composition are identical on both sides of an axis, for example, a knot garden or a butterfly's wings. A symmetrical design is often geometric and can appear static and safe.

An asymmetrical or informal balance occurs when the formal elements are arranged unevenly on either side of an axis. For example, a large shape can be balanced by a number of smaller shapes, or a large area of dark colour can be balanced by an area of fragmented lighter colour. Asymmetrical designs are usually more flowing, dynamic and stimulating.

A radiating or spiralling design is one in which the formal elements flow outwards from a central point, such as sunrays or a Fibonacci spiral.

Above *Beautiful Floral* (Rachel Lombard). Mixed-media appliqué with free machine embroidery.

Scale and proportion

It is important to consider the sizes of the shapes in your design and how they relate to each other and their background. The scale of the positive motif will determine the negative space around it; a large shape on a background can have a bold visual impact but can overwhelm the negative space around it, dominating the whole design. Conversely, a small shape on a background can be overwhelmed by the negative space surrounding it, making it appear 'lost'.

It is also important to consider scale and proportion in the context of the finished piece and its intended setting: a wall hanging may suit the proportions of a domestic space, but when hung in a public art gallery it may seem intimidated by the larger, formal space, lack visual impact and appear insignificant.

Above Impact of scale drawings (Julia Triston). This series of drawings shows the effect on the negative space when the scale of the motif is increased.

Below *And There Will Your Heart Be Also* (James Hunting) Hand embroidery on pieced linen, the work demonstrates a balance in scale and proportion and explores the relationship of each element, or motif, within space and each other.

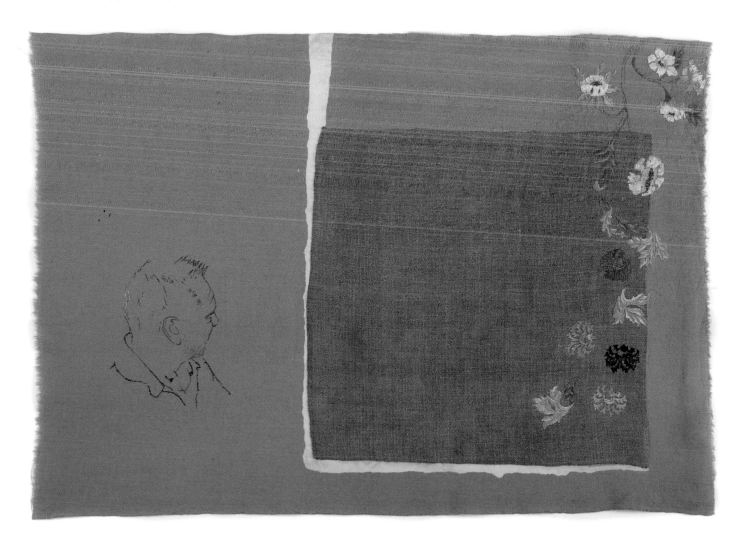

Emphasis and contrast

A dominant focal point is an area of a composition that your eye is drawn to; it adds interest to a design and attracts the attention of the viewer. Without a focal point, a design can be monotonous, restless and difficult to interpret.

A focal point is created by emphasizing one or more of the formal elements over another. This can be achieved most successfully by using contrasts in colours (tone/value or complementaries); shape (size, scale or proportion); line (type or direction); or texture (translucency/opacity or density).

Below *12 Happy Hearts* (Julia Triston). Colour and shape dominate this design; the use of red and green complementary colours draws your eye to the right hand side of the composition. Appliquéd silks on dyed cotton foundation fabric with free machine embroidery and hand stitch.

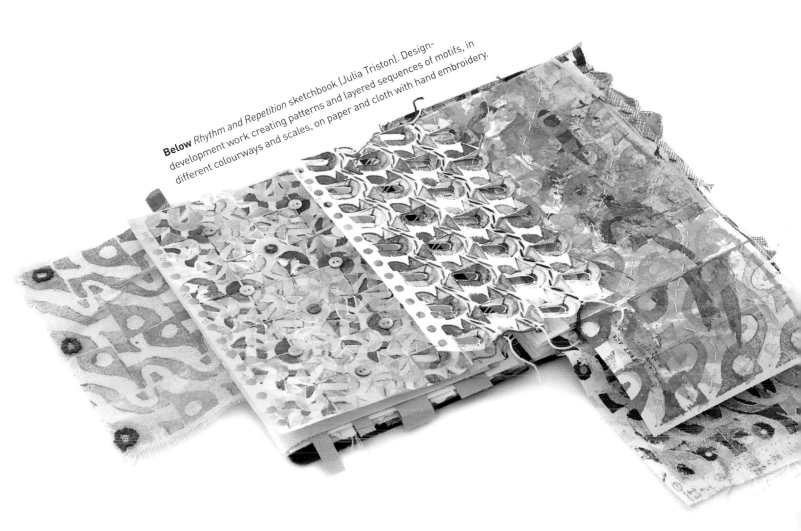

Rhythm and repetition

Rhythm within a design is created by organizing and repeating one or more of the formal elements to generate a sense of fluidity and movement across the surface of the artwork.

A contrast of lines and shapes, both actual and implied, will provide a variety of rhythm in a composition. Rhythm is needed to maintain visual interest and guide your eye around the piece; it is a dynamic way to create mood and can add excitement, liveliness, energy and tension to your work.

A sequence of repeated motifs will form a pattern. Patterns can be developed in simple or complex ways in lines, blocks, and half-drop pattern repeats to build a rhythm and a unity all over a surface.

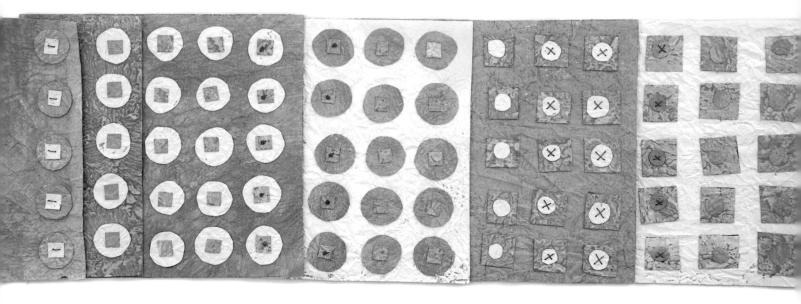

Unity and harmony

A piece of work that is unified and harmonious is not necessarily beautiful and easy on the eye – it can be discordant, uncomfortable and challenging to view; it depends on the aims and intentions of the artist.

To create a piece of work that conveys unity and harmony, all the elements and principles must come together to create a composition that has a sense of completeness and works as a whole.

Without unity and harmony, the individual components of a design will not work or belong together. Even if you want to place emphasis on one particular part of a design, the overall impact of the whole must be considered to achieve a sense of visual coherence.

The design elements and principles are the essential visual language of art and are equally important to each other. They are the fundamental visual communication tools, which will enable you to express your individual style and artistic voice with impact and creativity.

The process of analysing and applying the elements and principles will take time, but your knowledge and understanding will deepen with practice and experience.

Above Bonded paper experiments (Rachel Lombard). Papers bonded to papers, with minimal hand stitch, showing a unified repeat design.

Below Purse, 1980s, from Thailand (collection of Embroiderers' Guild). A symmetrical design showing unity and harmony; reverse appliqué in cottons with tiny 'invisible' stitches.

Conclusion to Part 2

Creating great design is a challenge that requires systematic thinking, planning and objectivity. Using the framework in this chapter will encourage you to think through what you are doing at every stage of design, and enable you to appreciate and critically assess your work and that of other artists.

In Part 3 we examine the fundamental skills and techniques required for making appliquéd artworks, and will outline the next practical stages for you to realize your designs successfully.

Below *Marshscape – Moonshadow* (Debbie Lyddon). Mixed-media appliqué collage with drawn-thread work, hand embroidery and machine stitch.

Appliqué: the basics

Materials and equipment

In this chapter you will gain an understanding of the types of fabrics and threads that are suitable for the more traditional styles of appliqué. This will allow you to approach projects more creatively. A comprehensive list of the appropriate tools and equipment for conventional techniques is also given. (Information on innovative textiles and contemporary tools and equipment for appliqué is set out in Part 4.)

Fabrics

Every fabric has its own specific properties, and understanding these will allow you to take advantage of their full potential, enabling you to make informed choices relevant to a chosen appliqué technique.

Foundation fabrics

A foundation fabric is the base layer upon which the applied work is stitched. This needs to be selected with care and must be appropriate for the style, purpose, scale and setting of a project.

A foundation fabric can be sturdy like canvas, or very fine like voile. It must be robust enough to be stitched into and substantial enough to take the weight of the applied fabrics and any decorative stitching and embellishments you may wish to add. For example, a different foundation fabric should be chosen for a parade banner, a child's dress or a cushion cover, as each has its own particular purpose, 'feel' and drape.

Previous page Jain canopy for house temple from India, early 20th century (detail) (collection of Julia Triston). Layered cotton and silk patches and strips stitched by hand onto a recycled foundation fabric. Exposure to sunshine has weakened and disintegrated some fabric patches, leaving fragments and stitch marks across the surface.

Appliqué motifs

The fabrics that will form the appliquéd design also need to be selected carefully according to the chosen technique, and are not usually heavier than the foundation fabric. The fabric(s) you choose need to be appropriate for the scale of the design and its intended use – for example a small-scale, intricate design would conventionally be worked in a finer fabric than a large-scale and bolder design.

Considerations when choosing fabrics for appliqué

There are hundreds of fabrics on the market – some will be more suitable than others for a particular technique and scale of project; others will be completely inappropriate! Taking time to select fabrics and understand their properties is a good investment, as hasty decisions may be regretted later.

The most commonly used and favoured fabric for appliqué is 100 per cent cotton because it is durable, washable, relatively cheap, easy to source and comes in a variety of weights and colours. It is easy to paint, print and dye, and is suitable for almost all appliqué techniques. Cotton is easily manipulated and will readily hold a crease or a shape when ironed or finger-pressed, which makes the stitching process easier.

Vintage fabrics, recycled clothing, second-hand household linens, old curtains and haberdashery remnants can be used for appliqué projects too. Collars, cuffs, ruffles and waistbands can be interesting embellishments.

Once you have decided what your appliqué project will be, as discussed on pages 28–31, you will need to assess potential fabrics for durability, fragility, washability, stability and longevity. Here is a checklist to help you:

Left Second-hand clothing (collection of Julia Triston). These shirts, skirts, aprons and old mattress covers are all ideal to recycle and re-purpose for motifs and backgrounds in appliqué projects.

Questions to ask yourself	Factors to consider	Action to take
Will the item be worn?	Fabrics must be comfortable.	Feel to make sure the fabrics will not be too stiff, scratchy or harsh against the skin.
Will the finished piece be handled regularly?	Fabrics must be durable.	Rub the fabrics with your fingers to check that they don't pill or snag.
Will the piece need to be washed?	Fabrics must be colour-fast.	Wash a sample piece of the chosen fabric with a sample piece of white cotton. Compare the two to the original fabrics to see if any colour has bled.*
	Fabrics may need to be pre-shrunk.	Cut two sample pieces, 15cm (6in) square, of fabric. Wash and dry one, then compare it to the unwashed square to check for shrinkage.**
Will the appliqué project be on display?	Most fabrics will fade in strong direct sunlight (some more quickly than others).	Cut two sample pieces, 15cm (6in) square, of fabric. Place one in a drawer and leave the other exposed to natural light for a few days (or weeks!), then compare results.
	Over a long period of time, most fabrics will begin to disintegrate in strong direct sunlight.	Taking the item off display or covering or storing it when it is not in use will help to extend its life.

* If the fabrics bleed, you may be able to wash out the excess colour, but if not you will need to choose an alternative fabric.

** If the fabric shrinks, pre-wash all of it before starting the project.

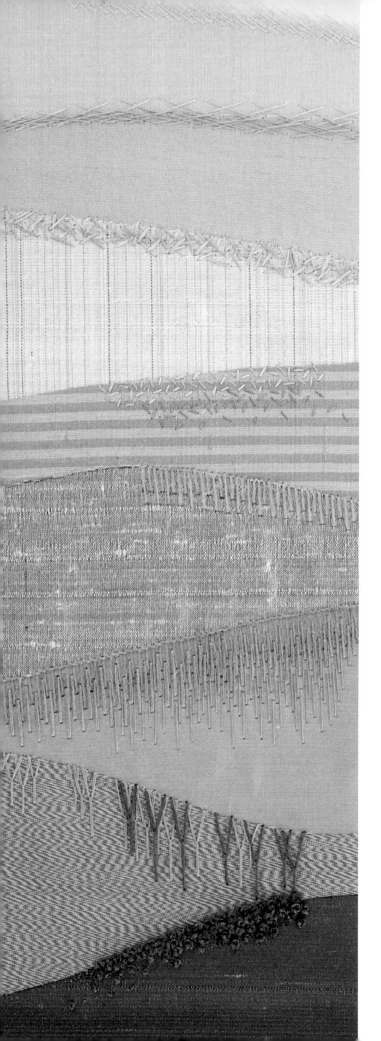

Threads

Lots of different types, colours and thicknesses of thread are suitable for appliqué. Some threads can be used for applying motifs, others to decorate an appliquéd surface, and some can perform both functions.

In hand-stitched appliqué, cotton or polyester cotton sewing threads are most frequently used to attach applied motifs. These threads are strong, and they come in a wide range of colours and different thicknesses – they are easy to handle and stitch with.

For machine-stitched appliqué, there are more thread options. Cotton and polyester cotton sewing threads can also be used on the machine and in addition, a wealth of specialist machine-embroidery threads are available.

These threads have many exciting qualities: they come in a vast array of colours, thicknesses and textures, and often have a lovely sheen and vibrancy – for example rayons and metallics. Specialist machine-embroidery threads are specifically designed for the mechanical process of stitching on the machine. They are not always suitable for hand stitching because they are finer, weaker, and so more likely to break and snag; they are also less durable than cotton and polyester cotton sewing threads.

Hand-embroidery threads, such as stranded cottons and silks, allow the possibility of combining the process of securing and decorating the motif at the same time – blanket stitch is the most commonly used stitch for this traditional method.

Hand and machine embroidery threads can also be used to decorate and embellish both the applied motifs and the foundation fabric to add highlights and emphasize some details of a design, if appropriate.

Left Appliqué sampler (Tracy A Franklin). Hand-embroidery stitches worked along the edges of bonded silk in tonal cotton and silk threads to create a landscape.

Above *Daisies* (Pat Sharples). Collaged scraps
and layers of leftover patchwork fabrics applied to
cotton backing with free-machine embroidery in
straight and zigzag stitching.

Tools and equipment

There are some key pieces of equipment that you will need for appliqué projects. Other items are optional – in time you will work out what is best for you and your individual practice. The list below is split into two sections – basic essentials for appliqué, and other more specialist items you may find useful as your knowledge and skills develop.

Essentials

- **Needles** There are many on the market and the ones you choose must suit your fabrics, threads and technique.
- **Sewing machine** Ideally one that does straight and zigzag (swing needle) stitch, and has the facility for free machine embroidery (see page 78).
- **Sewing machine accessories** Including machine needles, bobbins and suitable presser feet.
- **Scissors** Three pairs of *sharp* scissors are recommended: a sturdy pair for cutting fabric, a small pair for snipping threads, and a pair for cutting out paper patterns and templates.
- **Pins** There are different types available: choose pins that are an appropriate length and thickness for the weight of the fabric.
- **Stitch ripper** Useful for undoing seams and unpicking unwanted stitching.
- **Tape measure** One with metric and imperial measurements is useful.
- **Iron** Essential for smoothing and pressing fabrics.
- **Baking parchment (silicone based)** This can be used to protect fabrics from the intense heat of the iron, and to protect an ironing board or ironing surface.
- **Tailor's chalk** A valuable tool for marking out shapes and lines.
- **Hard pencil/fine liner** An alternative for marking fabric.
- **Thimble** Good to prevent sore fingertips, although some people never use one.
- **Embroidery hoop** This may be useful to stabilize foundation fabric when applying motifs, embellishments or decorative surface stitching by hand or machine.
- **Embroidery frame** Used for large-scale work (stitched by hand), this is free-standing and can be big enough for more than one person to work on.
- **Notebook/sketchbook and pencils** Essential for recording research, ideas, thoughts, plans, design development and the progress of a project.

Below A collection of some of the essential tools and equipment for appliqué and textile art projects.

Opposite A selection of specialist items and products which can be useful and time-saving when working with fabrics.

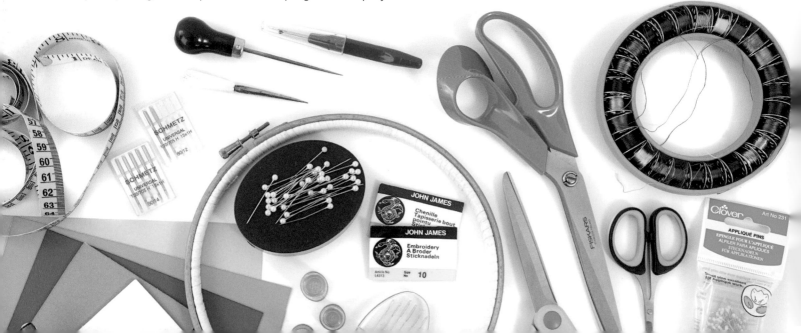

- **Papers** A range for patterns and templates, including tracing and tissue paper.
- **Thin card/plastic sheet** For making templates.
- **Tape** Masking tape or Sellotape to hold designs or fabrics in place.

Specialist items and products

- **Rotary cutter** A great sharp tool for cutting straight edges quickly.
- **Metal ruler** Essential for use with a rotary cutter, as one slip of the cutter will ruin the edge of an ordinary plastic ruler, or your fingers!
- **Cutting mat** A self-healing mat, with a marked grid on the surface, is useful for aligning, squaring up and measuring fabrics. A must when using a rotary cutter.
- **Quilter's ruler** Not cheap, but extremely useful for measuring out hems, corners, angles and parallel lines. Can be used with rotary cutters.
- **Tweezers** Useful for threading needles, picking up beads or placing small fragments of threads or fabrics upon a surface.
- **Pliers** Handy for pulling threads, wires or thick fibres through sturdy or bulky surfaces. Use one to pull a needle through thick fabric.
- **Bondaweb (Bondaweb 329, Wonder Under)** An iron-on, fusible webbing with a non-stick paper backing, used for permanently bonding two fabrics together.
- **Freezer paper** A paper which is 'waxy' on one side – placed waxy side down, this will adhere to fabric when lightly ironed. Useful for stabilizing fabric and for creating templates and stencils.
- **Stitch 'n' Tear** This is a fine Vilene, which can be put underneath a foundation fabric to stabilize it – particularly useful for preventing puckering whilst appliquéing on the machine (can be removed/torn away when stitching is completed, if appropriate).
- **505 Spray and Fix** A spray adhesive for fabric that is temporary and allows the repositioning of motifs; it is used to stabilize fabrics whilst stitching, and also helps to prevent fraying; it does not gum up needles.
- **Lapel Stick** A temporary fabric adhesive in stick form; does not gum up needles.
- **Carbon paper** For transferring designs on to fabrics.
- **Pounce powders** Fine powders such as cuttlefish bone, charcoal, flour, talcum powder or chalk, for the prick-and-pounce method of transferring designs.
- **Light box** A useful piece of equipment for transferring designs, but can be expensive.

Thinking about, choosing (then gathering together) fabrics, threads, tools and equipment is essential, and will be creative time well spent. Making the appropriate choices for your individual project will result in a more successful and original appliqué piece.

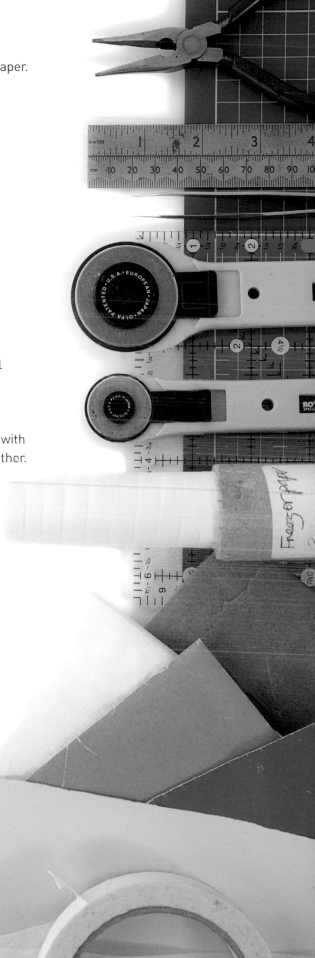

Transferring designs

This chapter sets out different ways of transferring designs to foundation fabrics. There are a variety of methods to choose from – select the one that is best for the fabrics you are going to use, and the scale and complexity of your appliqué project.

Once you have finalized your design, draw it out to scale on sturdy paper with a permanent pen, making sure that the outlines are strong and well defined.

This is your pattern, your original design reference and your working design. You may choose to colour it in, or add details of surface stitch or embellishments. The working design is not set in stone – you may find that it evolves as the project progresses. It is fine to change your mind and add, take away or amend some of the smaller details within the overall design.

It is important to transfer the main outlines and information from the working design to the foundation fabric to ensure that the finished appliqué piece successfully replicates the design you have worked out on paper. This will provide reliable reference points, boundaries and outlines to work within, and you can be confident that the design will work as intended. Finer details can be transferred at a later date.

It is important to mark the 'right' side of any copy of a working design, or elements of it, to avoid confusion when transferring the design to fabric and when cutting out motifs.

While there are other ways to transfer designs to foundation fabric, such as iron-on transfers, transfer pencils and vanishing marker pens, the methods we have focused on in this chapter are ones that we have tried and tested over the years and are the ones we most commonly use.

Transfer methods

Before you transfer a design, make sure that the foundation fabric is cut to size, includes an adequate seam allowance and is ironed or pressed so that it is smooth and flat. The foundation fabric also needs to be kept flat and still – with pins, weights or tape – so that it doesn't move about while you are transferring the design.

Freehand drawing

If you are confident enough and have a straightforward design, the easiest and most direct method is to draw the design directly onto the foundation fabric, by eye. Secure the foundation fabric to a firm surface (for example, a tabletop, with tape) and draw out the design with tailor's chalk or a hard pencil.

Tracing

If the foundation fabric is light in colour and thin enough, you will be able to see the design through it when the fabric is placed on top, so you can directly trace the design. Tape the working design to a firm surface (for example, a tabletop), place the fabric over it, smooth it out and secure it in place. Trace over the design on to the foundation fabric with tailor's chalk or a hard pencil.

If the working design doesn't show through the foundation fabric clearly enough, you may need a light source behind it – a light box, a lamp underneath a glass tabletop, or a bright window will all work well.

Templates and stencils

A template is a 'positive' design – you draw around the outside of a shape; a stencil is a 'negative' design – you draw around the inside of a shape. If you carefully cut out a template, you also have a stencil! They are usually made from thin card (for example, a cereal packet) or thin plastic (for example, an ice-cream tub lid). This is a good method to use when you want to transfer a small element of a design or a repeated motif – such as a leaf, flower, bird or letter – to a particular area of the foundation fabric. It is easy to add small details to a larger design as your work progresses, for example extra leaves on a tree. Draw around the template or stencil with a hard pencil or tailor's chalk.

Templates and stencils (Rachel Lombard) Simple motifs cut from thin plastic file dividers, showing positive shapes (templates) and negative spaces (stencils).

Carbon paper

Commonly used in dressmaking, this
is a paper with a coloured carbon
on one side – usually in red, blue,
yellow or white. The advantage of
this method of transfer is that
you can choose a colour of carbon
paper that will clearly show up on, and be
a strong contrast to, the foundation fabric.

The design and the carbon paper should be
cut to the same size as each other and
slightly smaller than the foundation fabric.
Pin the design and carbon paper together,
making sure that the carbon paper is
coloured-side down and the design is
facing upwards. Lay these two sheets, coloured carbon face down, on top of
the foundation fabric; because you can still see the edges of the foundation
fabric, it will be easier to place and align the design correctly. Secure all
three layers together with more pins, weights or tape. Draw over the design
with a pen or pencil and it will be transferred to the foundation fabric.

Above Carbon paper. A floral motif has
been traced around on top of red carbon
paper to give a strong outline on the
foundation fabric.

Tacking (basting)

This method of transferring a design to fabric is easy to
do, but it is more time-consuming than other methods.
Start by tracing the working design on to tracing paper
or tissue paper with a fine liner or a hard pencil. Lay
this tracing on top of the foundation fabric and pin it in
place. Using a thread that contrasts in colour with the
foundation fabric, hand-stitch over the lines of the design
using running stitches – use short stitches for small
designs and longer stitches for larger designs. Once
you have stitched over the design, very carefully tear
away the paper to reveal the outline of the design in
stitch. These stitches are permanent; they will stand
up to a lot of handling, will not smudge, fade or rub
off and will remain in place until you remove them.

Left Tacking. Running stitch shows up as a
guideline on the dark background as the tracing
paper with the motif on it is gently torn away.

Prick and pounce

This is an ancient method of transferring designs. It has been used throughout the world and is still popular today. In prick and pounce, a fine powder is pushed (pounced) through a pierced (pricked) design, leaving a dotted line on the foundation fabric. Traditionally, the powder used on a light fabric is charcoal, and the powder used on a dark fabric is cuttlefish bone. Alternatively, flour, talcum powder or ground chalk all work well.

You can use your original working design for this, or a copy of it – but whichever you choose, make sure the paper is fairly firm. With a sharp needle, pierce holes in the paper following the lines of the design, then lay this on top of the foundation fabric. With a rolled wad of soft felt, 'pounce' a fine powder through the holes. When the paper is removed, you will be left with a series of dotted lines; these can be joined up with a pencil line if necessary. For intricate designs, you will need to make sure that the pierced holes are very close together, otherwise the dotted lines will be difficult to follow and join up. For large designs, the piercing can be done with an unthreaded sewing machine.

Left Prick and pounce. The white powder shows on a dark ground when 'pounced' through the pierced holes on the tracing paper (left). The motif is transferred to the green fabric by pushing black powder through the holes to give a temporary outline (right).

Soap and net

This method is particularly suitable for transferring designs to dark foundation fabrics. Lay a pale-coloured piece of tulle netting over your working design and trace over the outlines with a permanent pen. Place this net on the foundation fabric and secure with pins. Draw over the pen outlines with a sliver of dry household soap – when the net is removed there will be a thin, definite and continuous line on the foundation fabric.

The table below is a guide to the best method to use for each type of fabric and style of design.

Fabric/design	Freehand drawing	Tracing	Templates and stencils	Carbon paper	Tacking (basting)	Prick and pounce	Soap and net
Light-coloured foundation fabric	✓	✓	✓	✓	✓	✓	
Dark-coloured foundation fabric	✓		✓	✓	✓	✓	✓
Patterned or striped foundation fabric	✓		✓	✓	✓	✓	
Intricate working designs	✓	✓		✓		✓	✓
Bold working designs	✓	✓	✓	✓	✓	✓	✓
Repeat motifs in working designs		✓	✓	✓		✓	✓
Large-scale working design*	✓	✓		✓	✓	✓	✓
Small-scale working design*	✓	✓	✓	✓	✓	✓	✓

* The scale of an appliqué project will have a bearing on the transfer method you choose. A large-scale project might be a curtain, a banner or a tablecloth, whereas a small-scale project might be a framed picture, a pincushion or a book cover.

Removing transferred marks

Left Soap and net transfer method. A sliver of soap is used to trace the motif through the net onto the dark foundation fabric.

You might want to remove some transferred lines because the applied piece does not cover the lines, or you have changed your mind, or you have made a mistake when originally transferring a design. It is important, however, to note that some transferred marks are much harder to remove than others, so it is always advisable to test out the method on your chosen fabric before you embark on a project. The table below gives guidance on the best way to remove transferred marks.

	Easy to remove	Hard to remove	How to remove
Tailor's chalk	✓		Rub, then wash.
Hard pencil		✓	Wash, but a trace of the line will probably still remain.
Carbon paper	✓		Wash away.
Tacking (basting) stitches	✓		Unpick with care.
Cuttlefish powder	✓		Brush off.
Charcoal		✓	Wash, but a trace of the line will probably still remain.
Flour	✓		Brush off.
Talcum powder	✓		Brush off.
Coloured chalk		✓	Wash away.
Soap	✓		Wash away.

Understanding, selecting and testing the most suitable method for transferring a design will give you the assurance to embark on projects with confidence.

Appliqué by hand and machine

The purpose of this chapter is to explain the technical basics clearly and to set out the essential skills needed for producing stitched appliqué by hand or machine.

Above *Beauty Mirror* (Rachel Lombard). Machine-embroidered collaged glossy magazine-paper background with applied printed silk slips.

Preparing fabrics

Make sure that fabrics for backgrounds and applied motifs are pre-shrunk (you may need to do this yourself), and iron them carefully so that they are smooth and flat.

Foundation fabrics

The size of the foundation fabric (the background) is determined by the scale of the design. Measure the working design carefully and add a generous seam allowance to this to calculate the size of the foundation fabric. It is a good idea to err on the side of caution and add a slightly bigger seam allowance than you think will be needed, as it is easier to cut this away than to add more fabric later!

For simple and traditional hand-stitched appliqué, plain cotton fabrics are most commonly used, as outlined on pages 50–53. Cottons and other woven fabrics have a grain; non-woven fabrics, such as leather and felt, do not. The foundation fabric should be cut along, and square to, the fabric grain so it will keep its shape and stability and be less likely to stretch and distort. Cut the fabric carefully to size with sharp fabric scissors or use a rotary cutter and metal or quilting ruler on a suitable cutting mat.

Transfer the design to the foundation fabric, if this is applicable, selecting the method most suitable for your fabric and design, as set out on pages 64–65.

Below Fabric grains. Aligning your grains will give a more aesthetically pleasing finish (left). Misaligned grains will be particularly noticeably on fabric with printed lines, or woven slubs (left).

Motifs

Wherever possible, motifs should be cut out so the grain of the motif will align with the grain of the foundation fabric when stitched. Aligning the fabric grains will give a better and more aesthetically pleasing result, and the motif fabric will then hang and move in the same way as the foundation fabric.

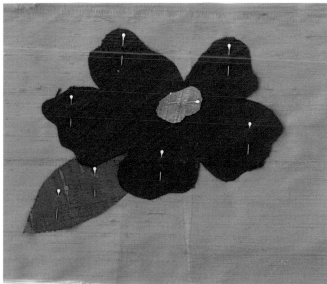

Stabilizing fabrics

There will be occasions when you want to combine fabrics with different weights, textures or finishes in an appliqué project. Thin fabrics (such as fine silks), or stretchy fabrics (such as jersey) may need to be stabilized to add body or prevent distortion, either for foundation fabrics or motifs. Fabrics can be stabilized by applying iron-on dressmaker's interfacing (Vilene); choose one to suit the weight of the fabrics, and use following the manufacturer's guidelines.

Hand-stitched appliqué

In hand appliqué, the stitching can be purely functional and virtually 'invisible', or be functional, 'visible' and decorative. The process outlined opposite is a logical way to approach any hand-stitched appliqué project.

Below These diagrams by Julia Triston illustrate how to clip seam allowances at corners and curves for fabrics that fray.

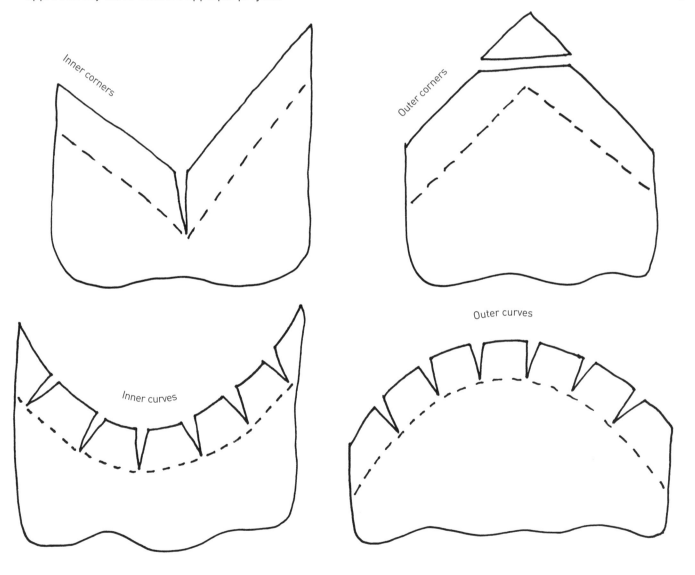

Preparing motifs for hand appliqué

Fabrics for motifs should be selected for the hand-stitched appliqué effect you want, and then prepared accordingly. Motifs for traditional hand appliqué, worked in cotton fabrics, are usually applied with small, 'invisible' stab stitches, whereas non-fraying fabrics are often applied with bolder, more visible decorative stitching.

Motifs cut from woven fabrics are likely to fray, so you will need to add a seam allowance to them. This added seam allowance needs to be measured more precisely and evenly than for the foundation fabric, as it is going to be turned under before stitching. Depending on how thick the applied fabric is, leave 6–12mm (¼–½in) seam allowances. The seam allowances will need to be manipulated for inner/outer corners and inner/outer curves – follow the instructions and diagrams opposite.

NB Take care when appliquéing a light fabric to a dark foundation, because if the motif fabric is too thin, the turned seam allowance will show through as a 'shadow' when stitched.

When cutting a motif from a non-woven fabric, such as leather or felt, there is no need to add a seam allowance as such fabrics do not fray.

Once prepared, position the motifs on the foundation fabric, aligning grains where applicable, and hold in place with pins or tacking stitches – keep these facing in the same direction to prevent the fabrics puckering.

Right Antique Hmong Tribe costume fragment (detail) (collection of Julia Triston). Hand appliquéd cottons intricately worked with tiny turned-under edges (on inner and outer corners) appliquéd with 'invisible' stitching.

'Invisible' stitching

This technique of hand appliqué is mostly used to stitch cotton motifs with turned-under edges to a foundation fabric. We recommend using stab stitches to secure motifs firmly – these stitches are small, neat, unobtrusive and straightforward to work.

Stab stitches are fundamental to the construction of the appliqué. When worked well, they will be virtually invisible, so the focus will be on the applied shapes and patterns rather than on the stitching.

Stab stitches are usually stitched 5mm (¼in) apart, but may be worked closer together on small or detailed motifs, and further apart on larger, less complex motifs. The spacing of the stitches should also be determined by the function of the appliqué project. For example, appliqué motifs on household linen will be washed more frequently than motifs applied to wall hangings, so these should be stitched more thoroughly and securely.

When stitching a motif to foundation fabric, use a thread that is the same colour as the motif, and about the same thickness as one strand of the fibres that make up the motif fabric: this will help to make your stitching less visible.

Select a suitable size of needle for the chosen thread – we recommend sharps for hand appliqué. Thread the needle with a length of approximately 45cm (18in). Whether you use a single strand, or double the thread for extra strength, always put a small knot in the end before you start to stitch. Begin stitching by bringing the needle straight up through the motif, very close to the edge. Then push the needle down into the foundation fabric at an angle, to tuck the stab stitch underneath the motif fabric. This will have the effect of almost rolling the edge of the motif under itself – and will ensure the stitches become as invisible as possible. There should be no stitching visible on the foundation fabric.

Once stitching is complete, secure the ends of the thread with a couple of small backstitches on the underside of the fabric, behind the motif. Then remove the pins or tacking stitches anchoring the motif.

Below Egyptian Tree of Life hanging (collection of Rachel Lombard). Egyptian cottons appliquéd with 'invisible' stitching with further decorative hand embroidery.

Visible stitching

This technique of hand appliqué is most commonly used for motifs cut from non-woven fabrics that don't fray, such as felt, but is also used with motifs that have turned-under edges. Visible stitching has a dual purpose – it holds a motif in place on the foundation fabric and forms a decorative stitched outline around it.

Blanket stitch and couching are the two most commonly used stitches in this style of hand appliqué, but other stitches may be equally suitable, as long as the stitch goes through both the foundation and the motif fabrics.

The structure, size and spacing of a chosen stitch should be even, regular and consistent. As your stitching will be visible and forms part of the design, it is important to choose a thread that either contrasts with, or complements, the motif and foundation fabrics. Any thickness and texture of thread can be used, as long as it can be stitched through the fabrics. The type of thread you choose will depend on the effect you want to create – for example if you are appliquéing scales on to a fish, you may choose to stitch with a glittery metallic thread, whereas if you are appliquéing petals on to a flower, you may opt for a matt cotton.

Choose an appropriate needle for the type of thread you have selected. We recommend using an embroidery needle or a chenille needle. Thread the needle – the length of the thread will depend on its quality and fragility. Some 'wear' and fray very quickly when stitching, whereas others are more resilient. Start with a small knot in one end of the thread, and once stitching is complete, secure the end of the thread with a couple of small backstitches on the underside of the fabric, behind the motif. Then remove the pins or tacking stitches.

Left *Play With Me* (detail) (Tilleke Schwarz). Hand embroidery on linen with small applied motifs, based on imagery and text encountered in everyday life (see page 26).

Far left Placemat, probably from the Philippine Islands, 1980s (collection of Embroiderers' Guild). Painted cotton appliqué motifs of flowers and leaves 'visibly stitched' to a shaped, fibrous foundation fabric – most likely pineapple cloth; blanket stitch in black thread.

Machine-stitched appliqué

In machine-stitched appliqué the stitching is always visible, so it is both functional and decorative. The process outlined below is a logical way to approach any machine-stitched appliqué project.

Preparing motifs for machine appliqué

Machine-appliquéd stitched edges can be either 'hard' or 'soft'. You will not need to add a seam allowance, but the type of edge you want can dictate the way you prepare the appliqué motif.

Once prepared, position motifs on the foundation fabric, aligning grains where applicable, and hold in place with pins or tacking stitches – keep these facing in the same direction to prevent puckering of the fabrics.

Hard edges

Hard-edged machine appliqué is stitched with a solid, strong and visible line of machine stitching. The stitching should completely cover the raw edge of the motif, which will prevent it from fraying; this is why there is no need to add a seam allowance. If you are cutting a motif from a fine or stretchy fabric, you may want to stabilize it first by applying an appropriate weight of iron-on dressmaker's interfacing (Vilene) to the reverse side of the fabric before cutting out the motif. This will help to prevent any puckering or distortion of the motif as you stitch.

To stitch hard edges, use either a wide zigzag stitch with a very short length, or a decorative machine satin stitch.

Choose a colour and type of thread that contrasts with or complements your chosen fabrics – see page 54 for further information. For the most even, smooth stitching, wind the same thread on the bottom bobbin as you are using on the top of the machine – this will also help to create an even tension and a much neater finish.

Begin by setting up your sewing machine – use an extension table if you have one. Make sure the machine needle is sharp, and is the correct size for the thickness of sewing thread and fabric weight. A needle size of 90/14 will suit most machine appliqué projects. When starting to stitch, bring the bottom bobbin thread up to the surface of the fabric: this will stop it from tangling underneath when stitching. On heavier fabrics, at the beginning and end of stitching, secure the threads with a couple of reverse machine stitches. On finer or more delicate fabrics, secure the ends of the thread by hand, by taking them through to the back of the fabric and darning into place behind the motif.

Right *Abstract in Appliqué* (Catherine Gowthorpe). Soft, bright cottons have been appliquéd to the foundation fabric with 'hard edged' decorative machine stitching. Some padded motifs and hand embroidery add further embellishment and contrast.

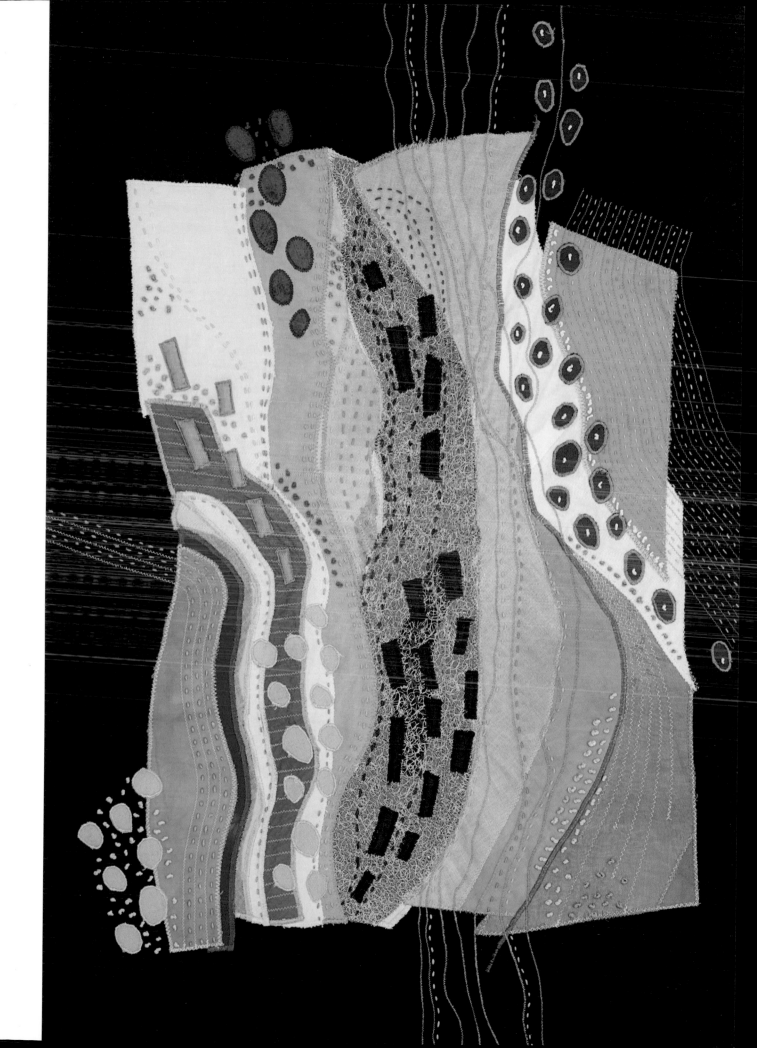

The width and length of the stitching will need to be worked out and practised on a sample of the chosen fabrics before embarking on the project. Remember that the stitching must evenly cover the raw edge of the motif – ideally, no motif fabric should be visible between the stitches. Generally, large motifs will require a wide zigzag stitch, and smaller or more delicate motifs will require a narrower zigzag stitch. Points, curves and corners of motifs need special attention when stitching: the stitch width should be narrowed and tapered towards points, stitches must be evenly spaced around inner and outer curves, and stitching on corners must join up and not overlap. As always, practice makes perfect!

Soft edges

Soft-edged machine appliqué is stitched with either ordinary straight stitch on the machine (for simple geometric motifs), or with free-machine stitching (for more complex, flowing motifs). There is no need to add a seam allowance, because the edge forms part of the decorative feature of this technique.

The motif is secured to the foundation fabric with a stitched line that is inset from the edge. This leaves a raw outer edge that is not covered or secured with stitch; a softened edge is created as the fabric fibres at the edge of the motif begin to wear and break down, or are left to flow and move freely.

Choose an appropriate colour and type of machine sewing or embroidery thread as discussed on page 54; this could either contrast with, or complement, the motif and foundation fabrics. As with hard-edged appliqué on the machine, your stitching will be smoother and more even if you use the same thread on the bottom bobbin as you use on the top – this will also help to create an even tension and a much neater finish.

Begin by setting up your sewing machine for your chosen way of stitching. Simple, angular motifs can be applied with a straight stitch and conventional settings – i.e. with a straight-stitch presser foot on and with the feed dogs up in the usual position. Use a stitch length appropriate to the size of motif being applied: select a longer stitch for large motifs, and a shorter one for smaller, more delicate motifs.

Below Edges sample (Rachel Lombard). Velvet ground with frayed chiffon squares applied under plastic with trapped threads and sequins.

Free machine embroidery

Complex, fiddly, or intricate motifs are easier to apply with free machine stitching, i.e. with a darning foot on and with the feed dogs down or covered. This technique enables you to 'draw' a precise, fluid and smooth line of stitch around the inside edge of a motif, without regularly stopping to raise the presser foot to turn corners. You also have the flexibility of changing the stitch length to suit the scale and design of the motif, as the stitch length is determined by how quickly or slowly you move fabrics under the needle.

Follow this checklist for setting up your sewing machine for free machine stitching:

Below *Time Tent*, visualizing the story of evolution (detail) (Victoria MacLeod). Cut-away appliqué motifs, applied to a layered background with free machine embroidery, leaving soft edges; further adorned with hand embroidery and embellishments.

- Drop or cover the feed dogs.
- Set the stitch length and width to zero.
- Fit a darning foot to the machine instead of a regular presser foot.
- Use the same weight of thread on the top and bottom bobbin of the machine.
- If you have a bobbin race, make sure the thread runs clockwise when unwinding.
- Use a sharp, new needle for each project.
- Place the foundation fabric in a bound 20cm (8in) embroidery hoop, if possible, or hold the fabrics taut under the needle (if using a hoop, make sure the fabric is touching the base plate – you will be stitching into what would be the back of the fabric if you were hand-stitching).
- Start stitching with the needle in the fabric; run the machine smoothly and evenly, and continuously move the fabric, or hoop, underneath the needle.
- Build up your speed gradually – jerky and sudden changes of direction, speed and tension can break threads and needles.

If you choose to free-machine embroider a motif in place, you may wish to go over your stitch lines twice – this creates a more defined line of stitching, holds the motif more firmly in place and makes it more durable (useful for items that will be regularly handled or washed).

Fabrics that don't fray may not need to be stitched along an edge to secure them – they could just be held down with some stitching in a pattern or in the centre of a motif with a knot.

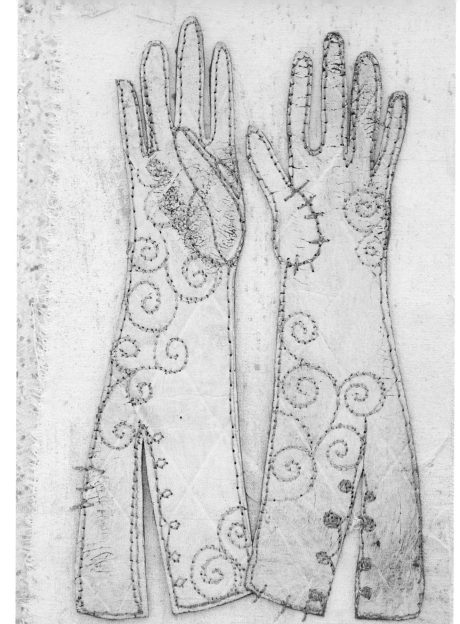

Above left *Flowers* (Thomasina Brown). Lazer-cut floral motifs from hand-dyed silk, attached to a cotton foundation with minimal free machine embroidery; this leaves most of the petals free standing to add an organic feel to the surface.

Above right *Glorious Gloves* (detail) (Priscilla Jones). Mixed-media appliqué panel.

For both conventional and free machine stitching, bring the bottom bobbin thread up to the surface of the fabric when starting to stitch, as this will stop it from tangling underneath.

At the end of stitching, loose threads can be cut off if they have been stitched over, but otherwise should be taken through to the back of the fabric and darned into place by hand behind the motif. Avoid reverse stitching if possible, as this can leave a lumpy 'mark' on an otherwise smooth line of stitch.

If you are initially uncertain about what type or style of edge you want, try them all out! Every fabric has a different property and will respond differently to each of the stitch techniques – do not assume that all fabrics will respond in the same way to the same technique.

Once you are confident with the basics of free-machine embroidery you can experiment with changing the tensions to create textural surface effects, such as whip, feather and cable stitching.

Using an embellisher

Appliquéd textiles can also be created using an embellishing machine. This looks and works like a sewing machine, but does not use any thread. Instead it has a number of barbed felting needles which, when moved up and down, 'push' fine fibres from the top fabric into the background fabric, and 'pull' the fibres of the background fabric through to the top. The two fabrics become 'dry-felted' together. This technique can be used to appliqué one surface to another loosely, or can be used to embed and integrate surfaces fully. The best fabrics to use for this technique are soft materials such as felt, scrim, fine silks and chiffons plus fibres and yarns.

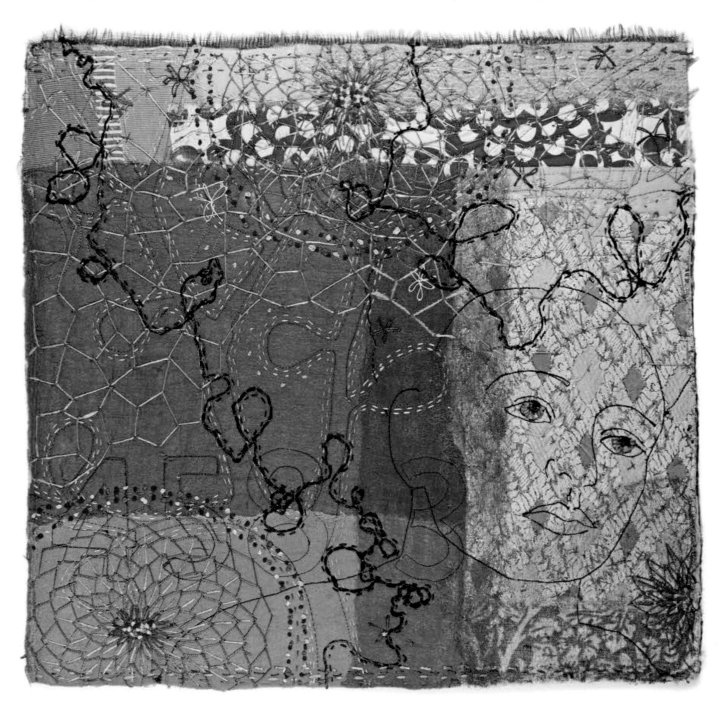

Above *One More Time* (Louise Baldwin). Various vintage fabrics have been patched and layered using the embellisher. Further imagery has been built up using both hand and machine stitch.

Left *Did we Really?* (Louise Baldwin). Patches of assorted recycled textiles have been pieced and appliquéd to the foundation fabric on the embellishing machine. Patterns and text in hand and machine stitch also secure the fabrics and further decorate the surface.

Conclusion to Part 3

In Part 3 we have looked at the materials, equipment, knowledge and skills needed to work traditional and non-traditional appliqué techniques confidently. Time spent sampling and testing materials, and practising and perfecting techniques will never be wasted – in fact this is crucial to the development and extension of your technical skills. In Part 4 we set out the breadth and depth of both traditional and innovative appliqué techniques and encourage you to experiment and discover new and exciting ways of working with, and combining, materials.

Part 4

From tradition to innovation

Appliqué techniques

This chapter will explain the most commonly used methods of appliqué. Each of these techniques has a set format and working method, and each is defined by its own distinct characteristics.

Once you understand the process and way to work each technique, you will be able to develop your own style and approach to it.

Previous page: Appliqué bag (detail) (Linda Archer). Rich and textured appliqué surface created by piecing and re-piecing assorted fabrics; densely stitched by hand and machine; adorned with buttons, sequins, beads and braids.

Left Blouse panel in mola work (early 20th century) (collection of Embroiderers' Guild). The top red layer is one complete piece that has been cut into as a stencil, depicting stylized animals; the edges have been rolled under and intricately and skilfully 'invisibly' stitched by hand on to a white cotton background.

Mola work

The word 'mola' means 'clothing' or 'blouse'; the technique is indigenous to the Kuna Indians of the San Blas Islands, off the coast of Panama and Columbia. Molas are geometric designs and usually symmetrical. They are created from layers of brightly coloured cotton fabric, which are traditionally stitched by hand. Mola appliqués are constructed using a combination of appliqué techniques. The basis of mola work is reverse appliqué. Traditional appliqué is used to add other motifs or designs to the background.

Above Blouse panel in mola work (collection of Julia Triston) from the San Blas Islands, worked in several layers of brightly coloured cottons onto a black background.

This technique consists of stacking layers of different coloured fabric, cut to the same size. Shapes are cut out of the upper layer(s) to reveal the colours beneath and raw edges are carefully turned under by 'invisible' hand stitching. Small 'patches' of contrasting coloured fabric can be sandwiched between layers and then exposed when the designs are cut through. This is done to be economical with fabric and to reduce the bulk and weight of the finished mola. Traditional appliquéd motifs may be inserted in empty spaces to enhance the multilayered effect further. Extra detail and colour is then added to the design with embroidery stitches.

Indian-style appliqué

Appliqué is a popular textile art form in India and neighbouring countries, where it is used to decorate clothing and traditional costumes, wall hangings and banners, household items, caparisons and howdahs. Frequently, appliqués are constructed from a combination of new and recycled fabrics and precious parts of old or worn-out textiles. Shisha mirror work and hand embroidery is often used to embellish and complete the appliqué piece.

Soft, plain cotton fabrics in earthy colours such as red, ochre, black and green are used for both motifs and foundation fabrics. Bold contrasting colours and the repetition of simple, stylized motifs make Indian appliqué designs both striking and effective. Commonly occurring motifs are applied flowers, and borders of triangles and bars. These are illustrated opposite – all are based on a folding and cutting technique which minimizes raw edges and simplifies stitching.

Very complex and intricate appliqué motifs can be created from one piece of cloth that is cut to form a stencil, which is then applied to the foundation fabric.

We recommend that you try out each method in paper first.

Flower motifs

1. Cut a rough circle out of the fabric to be applied.
2. Fold this circle in half and then into thirds.
3. Cut straight across the edge of the folded fabric to make all the edges of the motif the same.
4. Open the fabric out – you should have a hexagon – and make six incisions, the same length, in the middle of each straight edge.
5. Lay the cut-out shape on the foundation fabric, making sure the fabric grains are aligned, then pin in place. Turn small hems under and stab stitch as you go around the whole flower.
6. To cover the raw edges at the centre of the flower, cut out a smaller circle of fabric in a contrasting colour, and sew a line of running stitches around the edge. Draw up this running slitch to make a Suffolk puff (yo-yo), and secure your stitching.
7. Turn the Suffolk puff (yo-yo) over, flatten it and apply to the centre of the flower with small, neat stab stitches.

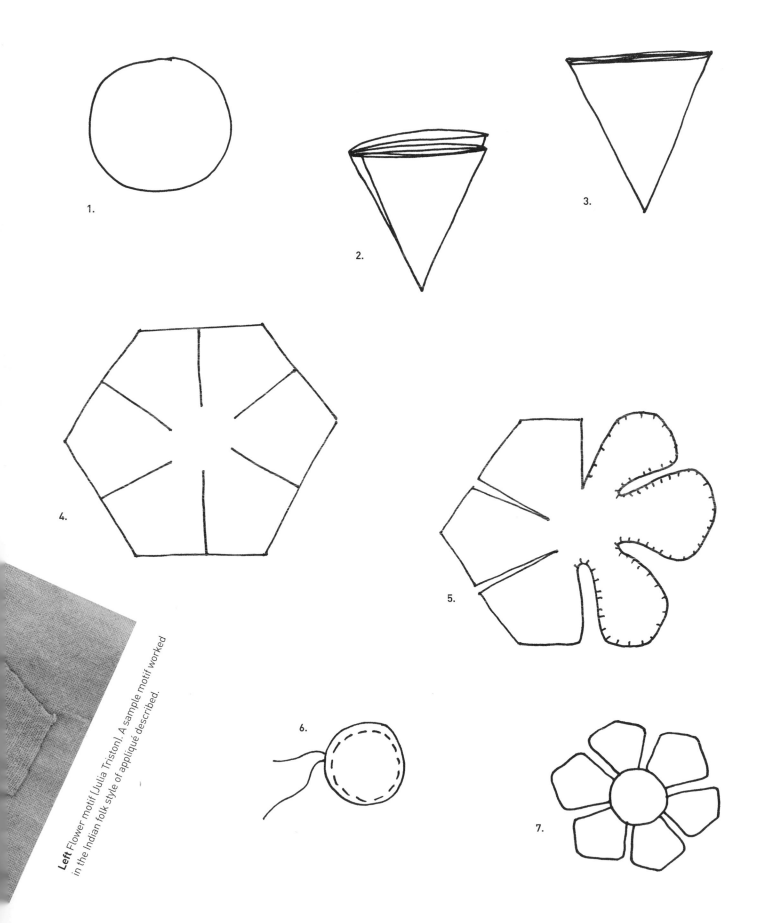

1.

2.

3.

4.

5.

6.

7.

Bars

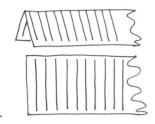

1. Cut a strip of fabric the length of the border to be applied (include a hem allowance).
2. Fold the fabric in half lengthways and cut several parallel incisions, an equal distance apart, then unfold.
3. Lay the cut bars on the foundation fabric and pin in place. Turn small hems under each bar, and stab stitch as you go around them.
4. A continuous strip of fabric or ribbon can be applied over the top and bottom of the stitched bars to neaten any raw edges.

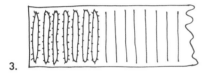

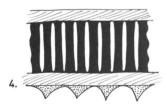

Stencil cut-outs

This technique can be as complicated as you choose to make it! If you are working with a large cut-out stencil, start by cutting out only the main areas; you can add the finer details by making additional cuts as your stitching progresses. Cutting out every little detail of a fabric stencil could make it too fragile and floppy to handle and lay in place successfully.

Be aware that the more complex a stencil motif, the more fiddly and time-consuming it will be to turn under the edges and stab stitch them to the foundation fabric. Remember to align the fabric grains and keep your stitches small, neat and regular.

Left Cushion covers from India (detail) (collection of Julia Triston). Both are worked with a matching top layer of fabric that has been cut out as a stencil and applied.

Above Appliqué bars (Julia Triston). This sample is partially worked to show the process of the technique described. This can be fiddly, but is very effective.

Triangles

1. Cut a strip of fabric the length of the border to be applied (include a hem allowance).
2. Cut into the fabric, at regular intervals, making straight incisions.
3. Fold each 'square' in half diagonally, then in half again on the opposite diagonal.
4. Turn the fabric over, so the folds are underneath, and lay the folded triangle border on the foundation fabric. Pin in place once the fabric grains have been aligned.
5. Work stab stich around the triangles carefully.

Below Triangles in borders on a variety of Indian textiles (collection of Julia Triston). A border of triangles is often used around the edges of garments, hangings and household textiles in India to outline or frame hand embroidery and appliquéd motifs. Here the triangles can be seen on both modern and antique pieces. Triangles can be shallow and wide, or tall and narrow, and are used on a variety of scales.

1.

2.

3.

4.

5.

Inlaid appliqué

Inlaid appliqué is a technique in which a positive shape is inserted into an identically shaped negative space, thus creating a smooth, flat surface, as the shape is inlaid *into* the fabric rather than being applied *on to* it.

This technique is most commonly worked in felt, as it doesn't fray, has a bit of 'give' in it, and has a depth to it. It is also possible to cut fluid and intricate designs from felt.

For this technique to be successful, it is essential that you use at least two contrasting colours of felt, and that you cut out the design very carefully, so that the shape and background remain as whole pieces. When worked accurately and precisely, you will end up with two or more pieces of inlaid appliqué.

The simplest form of this technique needs to be worked in the following order:

1. Select two pieces of felt in contrasting colours and two pieces of backing fabric (for example, fine cotton). All four pieces should be roughly the same size.
2. Transfer identical designs to both pieces of felt.
3. Very carefully cut out the designs from each piece of felt using small, sharp scissors. Remember to cut only along the lines of the design, so that the rest of the fabric remains intact. You will now have two positive shapes and two negative spaces.
4. Put the positive shapes into their opposite negative spaces to create an inlaid appliqué.
5. Lay each inlaid appliqué piece on the backing fabric.

Below left *Sri Lankan Elephant* (Rachel Clare Reynolds). Inlaid applique in felt, showing design placed and pinned to a foundation fabric ready for tacking in place.

Below right *Sri Lankan Elephant* (Rachel Clare Reynolds). Inlaid appliqué in felt, showing design securely tacked by hand to its foundation fabric.

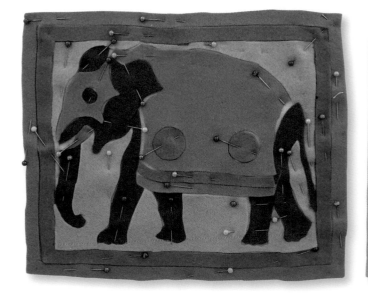 

6. On each appliqué piece, move and gently ease the positive inlay and its negative space to fit each other, so that the edges butt up neatly together and no backing fabric can be seen; pin or tack in place.

Right *Sri Lankan Elephant* (Rachel Clare Reynolds). Inlaid applique in felt, showing finished design complete with hand embroidery and embellishments.

Below right *Sri Lankan Elephant* (Rachel Clare Reynolds). Inlaid appliqué in felt, showing finished design stitched on the machine with hard edges, decorative automatic stitches and free machine embroidery.

7. To complete inlaid appliqués, you will need to secure them with stitch – these stitches are worked up through the backing fabric and over the join lines, securing the positive shape to its corresponding negative space (stitches can be decorative as well as functional).

Bonded appliqué

Bonded appliqué uses Bondaweb (Bondaweb 329/Wonder Under), with the heat of an iron, to fuse one piece of fabric permanently to another. Conventionally, small motif(s) are bonded to a larger background fabric and fabric grains are aligned. Bonded fabrics can also be used in a more spontaneous way to build collaged surfaces quickly and in a painterly fashion, as shown below.

Below *Cowboy* (Rhiannon Williams). Bonded coloured and patterned fabrics collaged in a fast and energetic way onto a cotton foundation. The absence of stitch conveys a strong graphic aesthetic.

This method of appliqué needs to be worked in a set order:

1. Iron the Bondaweb on to the back of the fabric from which the motif will be cut – keep its backing paper in place and remember to use baking parchment to protect the iron and ironing board.
2. On the backing paper, draw out the motif in reverse and carefully cut it out.
3. Peel off the backing paper and lay the motif – Bondaweb-side down – on the background fabric, aligning the grains if appropriate.
4. Cover with baking parchment and iron to melt the Bondaweb – this will permanently fix the motif in place. (NB Keep the iron moving and make sure that it isn't too hot, otherwise the Bondaweb may show through the surface of a fine fabric. For this reason, it is always a good idea to do a small sample piece first.)

Bonded appliqué is often used when fine, soft, or loosely woven fabrics (for example, muslin, scrim, fine cotton or silk) need to be strengthened and stabilized before they are cut into shapes and applied to a background fabric. Once backed with Bondaweb, fabrics become firmer, allowing complex and intricate shapes to be cut out.

The layer of Bondaweb also prevents the cut-out motif from fraying; there is no need to turn under the edges before applying the motif to the background fabric.

Depending on the purpose and function of the item, the edges of an applied motif can be left unstitched or decoratively stitched around with hand or machine embroidery.

Almost any fabric can be bonded to almost any surface – the only limitation is that the iron must be hot enough to melt the Bondaweb without melting the fabrics.

Above *Hagiography – to worship*. Graduate Collection 2013 inspired by religious imagery (Samantha Scott). Motifs from digitally printed fabric were laser-cut and bonded to a ground of gold lamé; a printed laser-cut outline and net hang over the top to create areas of light and dark.

Left *Bellowing Winds* (Rhiannon Williams). Bonded fabrics have been carefully cut, placed and ironed onto a background to build up a playful appliqué narrative, stitched with hand and free machine embroidery.

Broderie Perse

Broderie Perse (French for 'Persian embroidery') was a method of appliqué fashionable in seventeenth- and eighteenth-century Europe. This appliqué technique was originally a thrifty way of reusing (often imported) expensive printed fabrics, such as floral chintzes. Motifs were cut from these printed fabrics and then rearranged on a plain foundation fabric to form a 'new' design, which could be either pictorial or random in composition.

Above *Retro-style Flowers* (Beverley Holmes Wright). A composition of Broderie Perse appliqué from recycled fabrics, featuring free machine embroidery and machine-stitched patterns.

Left *Strippy Quilt Skirt* (Mandy Pattullo). Patched and pieced skirt featuring Broderie Perse appliqué detail, with hand embroidery and embellishments.

This technique is currently enjoying a popular revival as it fits the contemporary 'make do and mend' ethos of recycling and sustainability. Broderie Perse can be seen on clothing and accessories, in fashion and in interiors, where old fabrics have been 'upcycled' to create 'new' and revitalized items.

Motifs can be cut from furnishing fabric, household linen or clothing, and are either bonded to the foundation fabric or surface, or applied with hand or machine stitching. The design or 'picture' can then be further embellished with embroidery.

Cutaway appliqué

Cutaway appliqué (also known as reverse appliqué) is a technique that is most commonly stitched with free machine embroidery. A successful design relies on having strong shapes that can be outlined, or areas that can be enclosed, by stitch. This is an ideal technique for playing around with positive and negative designs (see page 39).

In this technique, layers of fabric are stacked up to form a pile that is stitched through. Selected shapes or areas are then cut away, close to the stitch boundaries, to reveal the fabrics beneath. All the layers can be of the same type of fabric, or you may choose to use contrasting weights, colours and textures. This allows you the freedom to be experimental, and occasionally surprised by your choices.

This method of appliqué needs to be worked in the following order:

1. Transfer the design to the top fabric, if you need to.
2. Layer the fabrics on top of each other, aligning the grain if applicable (you can stack as many fabrics as you want – as long as you can stitch through them).
3. Pin or tack the layers together, to prevent slippage when stitching.
4. Using free machine embroidery, stitch over the design two or three times. This gives better definition to shapes and outlines, and will prevent excessive fraying when the layers are cut away.
5. Cut away the chosen layers of fabric using small, sharp scissors.

Above *Flowers* (detail) (Ann Brookbanks). Free machine embroidered cut-away appliqué in cotton fabrics, with some motifs only partially revealed. A textured surface has been created with cut and folded-back layers, hand stitch, beads and buttons.

Shadow appliqué

In this technique, translucent or sheer fabrics are combined in layers in order to create a shadow effect and subtle changes in colour density across an appliquéd surface.

Shadows underneath

Traditional shadow appliqué uses layers of white cotton organdie, organza or net and is stitched by hand. This technique works best when bold and simple, rather than elaborate or intricate, motifs are used.

Select a suitable see-through top fabric, trace the motif on to this and put it into an embroidery hoop. Take a second piece of fabric, cut slightly larger than the size of the motif, and place this underneath the traced outlines on the top fabric. Make sure you align the fabric grains, then tack in place. Working from the top, carefully and neatly pin-stitch both fabrics together along the drawn outline. Once the stitching is complete, remove the shadow appliqué from the frame and then, from underneath, cut away the excess fabric around the edge of the applied motif, close to the stitched line, using small, sharp scissors.

Left Shadow work inspired by Hampton Court Palace (Tracy A Franklin). Embroidery worked on cotton organdie with cotton threads. Top: this shows the front of the completed piece, where the stitching and applied fabrics show through as shadows. Bottom: this image shows the reverse of the embroidery, where the detail of stitch and appliqué can be seen.

Shadows on top and between

This is a freer and more informal style of shadow appliqué. In this method, motifs are bonded or stitched to a foundation fabric and a transparent fabric is placed over the whole design to give an overall shadowy effect.

The transparent fabric is stitched in place, by hand or machine, around the edges of the motifs. It is important that the stitching goes through all layers of fabric and is secure, tidy and neat, as it will become part of the overall design. Different effects can be created by trapping motifs between two layers of transparent fabric.

Areas of the transparent fabric can then be cut away to reveal the brighter colours of the motifs underneath, in the positive or negative areas of the appliqué. Take care not to cut into the stitching when cutting away the transparent fabric.

Below *Three Flowers* (Kathryn McSweeney). Shaped fragments of cotton, metallic and sheer fabrics sandwiched between a top layer of tulle netting and a bottom layer of voile, held in place with free machine embroidery.

Above *Spinning in Cumbria* (detail) (Jessica Owen). Free machine embroidered cut-away shadow appliqué in calico and voile, layered over a printed ground.

Collage

A collage is an assemblage of different materials and the act of placing these in new contexts. The juxtaposition of found materials with bought, or old with new, whether haphazardly put down or carefully placed, can lead to unexpected textural relationships, adding interest to an appliquéd surface.

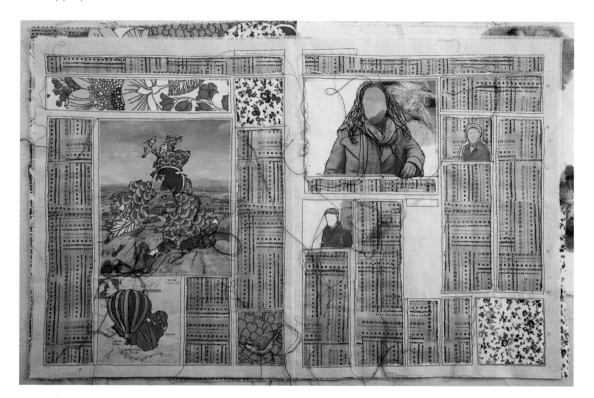

Left *Newsfabric 2*, based on a personal struggle with dyslexia (Alison Stewart). A textile framework, in the style of newspaper columns, has been collaged with fabrics and threads so that pattern and imagery give an alternative understanding to text.

Piecing and re-piecing

This style of appliqué involves covering the whole foundation fabric with similarly sized strips of fabrics in rows. These strips should be harmonious in colour but can vary in texture, and are usually secured to the foundation using decorative machine stitches. The whole piece is then cut up into squares or strips of equal sizes, placed in a different arrangement and then re-stitched on to a new foundation fabric. The process is repeated several times to create a dense and richly collaged surface, which can be further adorned with hand stitching and embellishments.

Above *Dowry Bag* (Yana Krizka). Re-pieced appliquéd silks and textured fabrics with decorative machine stitching and hand embroidery, adorned with beads.

Freestyle assemblage

This is a quick and easy way to create a textured, collaged surface with odds and ends and small scraps of fabrics, or other materials (for example, bus tickets, packaging or magazine papers). It allows you to explore combinations of colours and textures, and experiment with their scale and proportion.

Put the foundation fabric into a hoop (ready for free machining), and randomly scatter, or carefully place, small snippets of the chosen materials on the surface. Hold these in place with straight machine stitching – using either conventional or free-machine settings. It is easiest to work a small area at a time, adding to the collage as you go – otherwise the snippets will jump around as you stitch. The freestyle appliquéd surface can be used as a whole background or cut up into motifs.

Right Wedding bodice (embroidery by Julia Triston, construction by Joan Hutchinson). Central panel consists of tiny fragments of silks, velvets and metallic fabrics randomly stitched to a silk foundation with textured free-machine feather stitch.

Constructed backgrounds

Appliqué does not have to be the main focus of a design. Instead the technique can be used to construct a background for further stitch and decoration. Pieced backgrounds can be subtle, quiet and understated and can enhance, rather than detract from, any further surface stitching.

Three-dimensional appliqué

This is a general term for techniques of appliqué for which constructed, raised and padded motifs, or stuffed forms, are applied to a background to create textural interest, intense embellishment or a decorative focal point. Three-dimensional appliqué can be found on a wide variety of textile surfaces including lapels, hats, handbags and textile hangings.

Left *Corset in Flora* (Jane Rodgers). Boned corset in silk with appliquéd three-dimensional silk flowers.

Constructed motifs

In this method, shaped motifs are cut out and perhaps decorated with embroidery, beads, sequins, machine stitching, feathers or other embellishments before being applied to a textile surface as a finished decoration. They are held in place with just a few stitches, which may be either decorative (for example, French knots in the centre of a floral motif) or 'invisible'. Edges of motifs are usually left free and loose, to stand or flop, in order to create a three-dimensional, textured adornment.

Raised and padded motifs

Motifs can be padded with layers of wadding or felt to create a slightly soft and raised surface. In this method, the prepared motif should be cut out before the padding. The padding of wadding or felt must be cut smaller than the motif and laid flat. If you want to create a domed effect, more than one layer of wadding or felt can be used – in this case, each layer must be slightly smaller than the one underneath it. Once the layers of wadding or felt have been cut out and stacked, lay the prepared motif on top, turn the raw edges under if necessary, then stab stitch into place. The padded motif can be further worked with stitching or embellishments.

Stuffed forms

Shaped motifs of simplified flowers or animals can be stitched and stuffed with wadding, kapok or similar, to make them into three-dimensional forms before being applied to a background. Simple geometric shapes can be stitched and stuffed to create regular forms. For example, circles of fabric can be gathered and stuffed to create puffs; rectangles can be sewn and stuffed to make tubes; triangles can be formed into cones. There are many ways of doing this and the possibilities are endless!

Sculptural forms

Constructed textiles that are designed to hang, stand alone, or be played or interacted with can also incorporate appliquéd surfaces as part of their overall design. In three-dimensional pieces, even though the appliqué is an integral part of the decoration, the emphasis remains on the sculptural form.

Right and below *Blue Budgie* and *Green Budgie* (Karen Suzuki). Three-dimensional (life-size) sculptures formed from stuffed textile base with wire in legs and tails; decorated with patches of appliqué from re-worked fabrics to create surface texture and pattern.

Right *Hazel* (Joanne Edwards). Three-dimensional jewellery created with manipulated and layered felt forms and woollen embellishments.

So far, we have explained some of the most widely used and recognized styles of appliqué. It is essential to understand and master the basics of these techniques before you begin to explore and develop more creative and innovative ways of working.

In the next section, we will show you how, through discovering and working with non-traditional materials, you can break the rules and push the boundaries to make unique, original and contemporary appliqué artworks.

Left *Textural Pigeon* (Karen Suzuki). Three-dimensional (life-sized) stuffed form with collaged surface appliqué stitched by hand; the raw fabric edges create a fitting texture for the subject.

Pushing the boundaries

We have already examined traditional, well-established styles and techniques of appliqué and set out the standard ways of working each method. here we explore innovative and creative approaches to appliqué, and encourage you to push the boundaries to make individual, expressive and contemporary appliqué work.

Once you have mastered the basic principles of appliqué, you can begin to explore and experiment with alternative materials – challenging yourself as a maker, and challenging those who view and use your artwork.

It is great fun to play with and test the possibilities of different materials in order to explore their qualities and properties; however, always keep it in mind that a finished item needs to be fit for its intended purpose. This means that any combination of materials you choose to work with must be tested and sampled appropriately.

Above left *Far Away* (Rachel Lombard). Painted and stitched paper with applied dyed paper curl and leaf.

Left *Far Flung* (Rachel Lombard). Painted and pieced stitched paper with applied dyed paper leaves, machine-stitched curls and beads.

Specialist fabrics

There are many specialist fabrics that have a specific and traditional purpose; for example sinamay is used to create form in millinery, and interlinings and interfacing are used to stiffen and strengthen fabrics in dressmaking. But specialist fabrics can also be used in non-traditional ways for contemporary appliqué projects. With some imagination and experimentation, exciting and innovative surfaces can be developed. You could investigate:

- Interlining and interfacings
- Fun furs
- Furnishing fabrics
- Brocades
- Polar fleece
- Tyvek
- Abaca tissue
- Coloured foam sheets
- Silk carrier rods
- Carpet underlay
- Bandages
- Sinamay
- Netting and tulle
- Towelling
- Scrim
- Hessian
- Leather
- Lace, ribbons, tapes and other haberdashery items

Left *Tower* (Emily Hall). Bonded and lazer-cut fabrics (leather, denim, taffeta, silk jersey) layered on silk chiffon to create surface texture, movement and structure; minimal hand stitch with some pigment screen printing.

Unusual materials

In addition to specialist fabrics, many everyday items can be imaginatively recycled to create surprising or unexpected appliquéd surfaces, such as:

- Latex and rubber gloves
- Inner tubes
- High-visibility clothing
- Dusters
- Old tent fabrics
- Underwear
- Tea towels
- Tights
- Old wetsuits
- Aprons

Look around and see what you can find in and around your home, garden, shed or office – you may make some intriguing discoveries.

Left *Fold in Fold out* series (samples for garments) (Sarah Dyer). Lazer-cut motifs applied by hand onto plastic foundation fabrics.

Above Contemporary appliqué sampler (detail) (Jamie McGarvey). Plastic, neoprene and metal appliquéd motifs; applied to a polyester background with French knots.

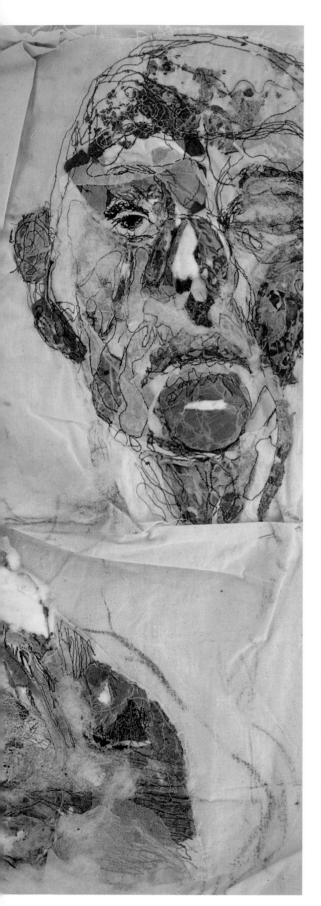

The table below lists further materials that are not traditionally used in appliqué, which can be used creatively in a contemporary context.

Plastics	Carrier bags • Florist's paper • Cellophane • Sweet wrappers • Packaging • Plastic sheeting • Storage bags • Files and wallets • Ice-cream and margarine tubs • Blister packs • Body scourers • Foam sheets • Shower curtains • CDs • 'Foil' blankets • Acrylic sheets
Papers	Fibre papers • Money • Flour or sugar bags • Animal-feed sacks • Tea bags • Thin card • Magazine pages • Kitchen towels • Wallpapers • Maps • Newspapers • Book pages • Doilies • Sandpaper • Wrapping paper • Brown paper • Paper cake cases • Tissue paper • Old envelopes • Tracing paper
Metals	Milk-bottle tops • Tinfoil • Foiled packaging • Chocolate wrappers • Shims • Wire forms • Scourers • Drinks cans • Foil lids from yoghurt pots • Tomato purée tubes • Found rusty metal pieces
Organic and natural materials	Plant leaves • Bark • Petals • Dried flowers • Coconut matting • Feathers • Onion skins • Corn on the cob husks • Thin cork sheets • Balsa wood • Sponges • Loofahs

You can determine, through careful experimentation, what each material can and cannot do, and which is suitable, or not, for your contemporary appliqué project. First, learn about the properties of non-traditional material(s) and consider them in terms of:

- **Texture**
  Is it soft or hard?
  Is it rough or smooth?
  Is it shiny or matt?
  Is it reflective?

- **Density**
  Is it thick or thin?
  Is it loosely woven?
  Is it non-woven?
  Will it fray?
  Is it brittle?
  Is it firm?
  Is it flexible?

- **Colour**
  Is it a bold or a subtle colour?
  Is it its original colour or has it faded?
  Is it naturally coloured or artificially dyed?
  Is it opaque or transparent?

It is also important to explore the potential of non-traditional materials. Ask yourself what you can make each material do.

Will it tear and/or cut?
Can I fray it?
Will it stretch?
Will it shrink?
Will it bend?
Will it scrunch?
Will it roll or flex?
Can I stitch it by hand and/or machine?
Will it hold a fold or crease?
Can I layer it?
Can I pierce or puncture it?
Can I drill into it?
Can I paint or dye it?
Can I burn it?
Can I distress or distort it?
Can I manipulate it?
Can I bond or fuse it to itself or another surface?

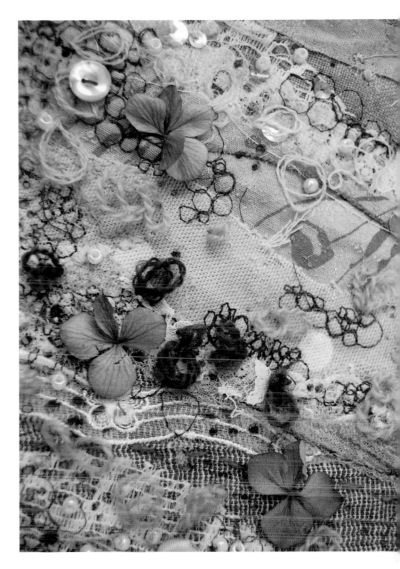

Opposite *Decay* (Dave Tweedy). Contemporary appliquéd shroud with papers, leaves, fabric and free machine embroidery onto calico ground.

Above *Flourish* (detail) (Emily Notman). Bonded, stitched and burned appliquéd surface with natural and hand-made embellishments.

One of the exciting parts of this process is the opportunity for your work to be materials-led – the exploration of materials can inspire new starting points for designs. The process of playing, testing and sampling will develop your understanding of the possibilities and limitations of materials. It will be an ongoing journey of discovery and not everything will work: you will have some great successes and you may have some disappointing results. It is important to record all your experiments so you can replicate successful outcomes.

Breaking the rules

When pushing the boundaries of appliqué techniques, it is important to realize that as well as different types of fabrics and materials, you can also experiment with alternative ways of attaching, applying and securing one 'material' to another. Moving beyond using just traditional stitch and bonding methods is all about breaking rules – it can enable you to produce exciting and innovative artwork that challenges the preconceptions of what appliqué is.

Contemporary appliqué can be stitched by hand or machine. Both have distinct characteristics, but hand stitching can often be more flexible; considerations such as the scale and size of a project or the thickness, weight, flexibility and stiffness of materials may limit the stitching that can be done by machine.

Stitching by hand

There are a myriad of hand embroidery threads commercially available (such as stranded cottons, knitting yarns and floss) – all can be used creatively in appliqué. The scale, tension, texture and length of stitch can be played with. Stitches can be loopy, knobbly, knotted, overlaid, paired, whipped, wrapped, embellished, woven and manipulated.

Below Pocket (detail) (Julia Triston). Leather jacket pocket featuring leather floral motifs appliquéd with dental floss and cassette tape.

There are also many 'alternative' threads suitable for hand stitching. These can be found in a range of colours, textures and finishes and can enrich and enliven your work. Many of these can be sourced from around the home, or are easily recycled. The list below is not exhaustive, and gives some suggestions to try out:

From the house	Cassette tape • Dental floss • Shoelaces • Fine jewellery chains • Packing tape • Paper string • Plastic carrier bags • Pipe cleaners
From the shed	Wire • Fishing line • Garden twine • String
Natural fibres	Hair • Grass • Raffia • Jute • Thin, flexible twigs
Haberdashery items	Torn fabric • Leather thonging • Lace • Ribbon • Cord • Braid • Elastic

Alternative needles

If you choose to experiment with unusual materials and alternative threads, you may find that a conventional sewing needle is unsuitable, as the eye may be too small to thread. Also, ordinary needles may be too short, too fine or too weak to pierce a 'fabric' or pull a 'thread' through when stitching.

There are several specialist needles on the market designed for specific stitching jobs, such as chenille needles, curved needles, mattress needles, leather needles, big, chunky darning needles and bodkins.

If you are unable to find a suitable needle for experimental appliqué work, improvise by making your own alternative 'needle' from a coffee stirrer, a safety pin, a piece of bent wire or a fid (see Glossary, page 122) ...

Stitching by machine

When selecting sewing threads for the machine there is a huge and exciting range of colours, textures, weights and finishes to choose from, including metallics, rayons, variegated and buttonhole threads – see page 54. Most are suitable for both conventional machine stitching and free machine embroidery.

When stitching on the machine, you don't have to stick to the conventional use of straight stitch, zigzag and basic free machine embroidery. There are many innovative ways to machine-stitch appliqué – here a few ideas:

Below *Coloured Lines* (detail) (Julia Triston). Linear appliqué sample experimenting with the tailor's tacking foot on the machine, to create surface texture.

- Experiment with different stitch lengths.
- Change machine tensions to create whip, feather and cable stitch.
- Explore set decorative or standard utility stitches.
- Try using a twin, triple, wing, or twin-wing needle.
- Play with different machine feet, such as a braiding foot or a tailor's tacking foot.
- Stitch with two threads through a single needle.
- Mix different types and styles of stitches together.
- Combine contrasting textures and thicknesses of threads.

It is worth noting that there are universal machine needles, which are suitable for most machine-stitched projects. There are also needles made for specific stitching tasks such as quilting, machine embroidery and stitching with metallic threads. Other needles are manufactured for stitching fine or delicate, and heavy or robust, fabrics – these include ballpoint and microtex needles and jeans/denim and leather/vinyl needles.

Your stitching will be smoother and more enjoyable if you choose a needle that is appropriate for your fabrics and threads.

Cutting and piercing to make holes

If you choose to work with a very thick, stiff, unyielding, dense or hard surface, either for the foundation 'fabric' or appliqué motif, you will need to think about how you are going to apply one to another. If you are going to use stitch, you will need to pierce or make holes in the surface(s) first.

The size of the piercing or hole needs to be considered alongside the 'thread' you will be using; the piercing or hole can be a feature in itself, or made just large enough for the thread to pass through.

A piercing can be used to push tough fibres apart, for example in thick canvas, whereas making a hole will cut and remove part of the 'material', which is necessary when stitching through wood and some plastics.

Holes can be regularly or irregularly spaced, big or small, shaped to suit your design, subtle or made into a feature, used singly or in clusters, used to create a pattern along an edge ... there are many exciting possibilities to explore.

Piercings and holes can be made/cut with several different implements, including the following:

- Scissors
- Craft knife
- Hole punch
- Drill
- Bradawl
- Stiletto
- Soldering iron
- Spiral punch
- Lazer cutter

Remember that the pieces you have punched out or cut out can be used in your design and stitch work too. Always work on a firm, protected surface when piercing or cutting materials.

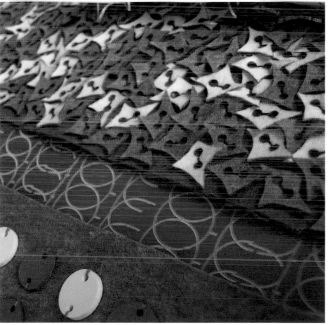

Top *Purple Elephant* (Julia Triston). Cut-away appliqué with soldering iron; on voiles and Kunin felt with free machine stitching in metallic thread.

Above Pierced motif samples (Kat Cullen). Regularly shaped industrial felt motifs, formed on the lazer cutter, stitched onto a background to build pattern and texture; held in place with hand stitch.

Non-stitch

As well as appliquéing with stitch, there are alternative ways of securing one surface to another. Some methods are permanent, while others are more flexible and interactive. Some non-stitch methods will change the feel of a surface, and could make subsequent stitching (if appropriate) more difficult.

Adhesives

Some 'materials' can be 'appliquéd' together with glue. There are many types of glues on the market – some multipurpose; some for specific materials and tasks. It is vital to test glues on 'materials' thoroughly before you embark on a project. This will give you an indication of drying times and any adverse effects or staining on surfaces. You may need to test a few different glues before you decide on the most suitable for a project. Here are some that we use:

- **Pritt adhesive stick** Useful in paper appliqué projects.
- **505 Spray and Fix** A temporary spray-on adhesive for fabrics.
- **Lapel Stick** A temporary fabric adhesive in stick form.
- **Wallpaper/cellulose paste** Useful for collaging together large areas of mixed-media work.
- **Emulsions and gels** These act like a glue when painted over the surface of fabric or fibres.
- **Polyfilla** Made up to a sloppy consistency, this is a great binder for mixed-media work.
- **Glue gun** A great tool for bonding two sturdy or non-porous surfaces together, such as rubber and cork.

Some materials have a sticky back to them already – such as tapes, plastics, foams, stickers and postage stamps; these can be stuck to a surface and many can be stitched into to form part of a design or an arrangement in a background.

Left Non-stitched appliqué motifs (Jamie McGarvey). Motifs from lazer-cut suede, backed with cotton high-visibility polyester fabric and voile, have been applied onto a silk ground with minimal machine stitching to allow the motifs to move with the flow of the fabric.

Right *Hagiography – to worship*. Graduate Collection 2013 inspired by religious imagery (Samantha Scott). 'Negative' motifs from laser cut digitally printed fabric (see page 93) were bonded to a ground of gold lame and net. The layered design, for fashion garments, has been constructed without stitch.

Fusing

An exciting alternative to stitched appliqué is to fuse one surface to another with heat. Bonding, melting, laminating and welding unusual materials with heat tools can be fun and produce innovative and sometimes surprising results.

There are several different products used to fuse materials and surfaces together; here are a few that are commonly available:

- **Bondaweb** As discussed on pages 92–93, this is used to permanently fuse one surface to another.
- **Misty Fuse** A very light and sheer fusible webbing.
- **Bonding powders** These have similar properties to Bondaweb and can be sprinkled on the surface in specific areas.

Such products rely on heat from an iron to melt them in order to bond the surfaces together. Be aware that if the surfaces are very thick or dense, the heat may not penetrate well enough to melt the fusible product and form a strong, permanent bond.

Heat tools can also be used in unconventional and more imaginative ways:

- **Household iron** A dry iron, or one with the steam setting turned off, is ideal for laminating, melting and permanently bonding some plastic surfaces together; areas of one colour can be cut out and used as a motif on another coloured plastic. Always protect the iron (see Health and Safety).
- **Soldering iron** Use this to fuse synthetic fabrics together; when the soldering iron comes into contact with the top layer of fabric, it will melt it and weld it to the layer of fabric beneath – lovely marks, holes and patterns can be drawn into the surfaces, and motifs can be cut out with the soldering iron and reapplied (see Further Reading).
- **Heat gun** This can be useful for fusing and laminating plastics, cellophanes and some synthetic fibres together. It is less controllable than using an iron but can create interesting textured effects (see Further Reading).
- **Laminator** A handy tool for quickly and simply encasing pre-designed motifs, or bits and pieces that can then be cut out to form motifs. A great contemporary alternative to traditional shadow appliqué.

Above and opposite *Flat-pack Dresses* (Sarah Morbey). From left to right: 'Clear Polypropylene Printed Dress Front' over 'Blue Vinyl Dress Front'; 'Sublimation Milk Top (1)' and 'Clear Polypropylene Stitched Dress Front' layered over 'Nude Vinyl Printed Top & Skirt Combo'; 'Mesh and Metal Dress Front'. Garments constructed from heat-set, printed and stitched reclaimed waste fabrics (including vinyl, polypropylene, milk-bottle tops, plastic bags, anti-slip mat and reclaimed metal), fastening with Velcro tabs.

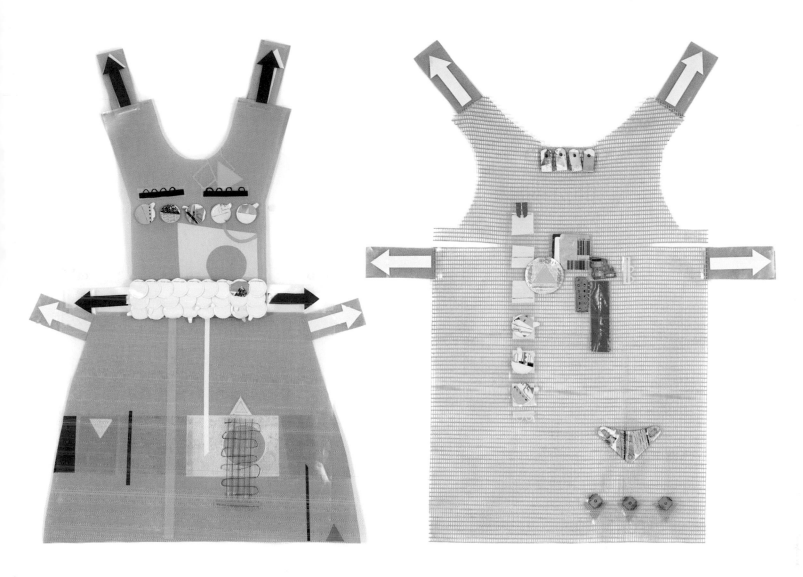

Health and safety

Although experimenting and playing with heat tools can be fun, it is important to bear in mind health and safety considerations. Using tools and materials in unconventional ways in a domestic or workshop setting may pose risks. Please follow the guidelines outlined below:

• When fusing, melting and bonding surfaces together, fumes can be produced – make sure you work in a well-ventilated area, or outside if possible.
• Buy a respirator if you are working with materials that could give off toxic fumes – and wear it.
• Follow all manufacturers' guidelines for products and equipment.
• Protect work surfaces properly.
• Always use a top and bottom layer of baking parchment to protect a domestic iron and ironing board when using Bondaweb or ironing plastics (this may stick to fused layers, but will peel off easily when cool).

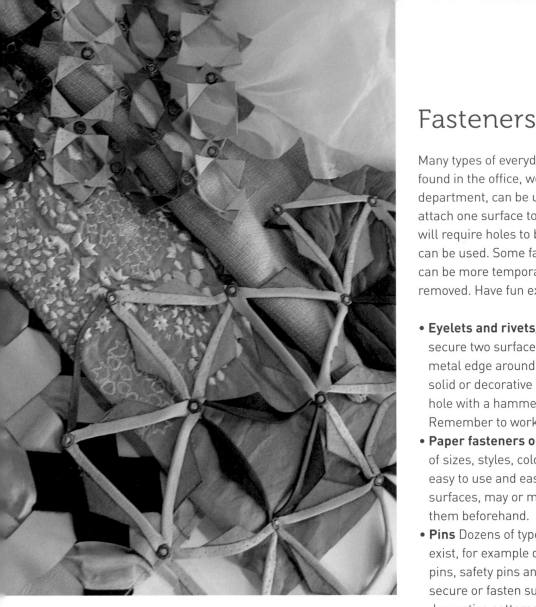

Fasteners

Many types of everyday and specialist fastenings, found in the office, workplace, or a good haberdashery department, can be used unconventionally to join or attach one surface to another. Some of these fastenings will require holes to be pierced or punched before they can be used. Some fastenings are permanent; others can be more temporary, but may leave a mark or hole if removed. Have fun experimenting with the following:

- **Eyelets and rivets/studs** These will permanently secure two surfaces together. An eyelet creates a metal edge around a hole, whereas a rivet/stud has a solid or decorative cap. Both are set through a punched hole with a hammer or specialist tools (bought in kits). Remember to work on a hard surface.
- **Paper fasteners or brads** These come in a wide range of sizes, styles, colours, shapes and lengths; they are easy to use and easy to remove and, depending on the surfaces, may or may not require a hole to be made for them beforehand.
- **Pins** Dozens of types of decorative and functional pins exist, for example dressmaker's pins, glass-headed pins, safety pins and kilt pins. All can be used to hold, secure or fasten surfaces together, perhaps in decorative patterns.

Above:
Contemporary appliqué samples with fasteners (Sophie O'Brien). Eyelets and rivets attach folded grids and strips of leather to assorted fabric backgrounds, forming layered appliquéd frameworks.

- **Nails and tacks** Use these creatively to apply firm surfaces to each other, such as balsa wood and strong leathers. Some have decorative heads, but remember that they may add considerable weight to your artwork.
- **Bulldog clips and pegs** From big, chunky and utilitarian to small, delicate and pretty – motifs can be clipped in place on a heavily textured surface or along an edge or corner, or through a preformed hole or slot such as a buttonhole.
- **Nylon tags** These require a tagging gun used for labelling clothes. These days they are often used in quilt-making to hold layers of fabrics together, but can also be used in exciting ways in contemporary appliqué.
- **Ties** A quick and extremely versatile way of securing one surface to another. There are many ties to play with, such as treasury tags, freezer-bag ties and plant ties. They can loosely attach a motif to a foundation, or be pulled tight to hold surfaces closer and more firmly together.

All of the above fastenings can be used to create patterns along joins and edges. They can be used singly as one point of attachment, or in groups, or used in conjunction with each other. They can secure small or large motifs and can also be a decorative feature in their own right.

Detachable fastenings

It is possible to use haberdashery items to attach appliqué motifs to background surfaces. Each of these has, or needs, two parts to be functional, but all have the advantage of enabling a motif to be detachable or interchangeable.

- **Buttons and buttonholes** Buttons come in a never-ending range of sizes, shapes, colours, patterns and materials (you can also make or cover your own). Buttonholes can be a slot that is slashed or finished by hand or machine; each can be a bold feature or neat and discreet.
- **Poppers and press studs** These can be metal or plastic and come in a range of colours, finishes and sizes, in pairs or in strips; stitch on or rivet in place.
- **Hooks and eyes** These are available in different sizes, weights and shapes, in pairs or on strips; stitch on to create a feature or hide behind the motif.
- **Bra clips and suspender clips** An alternative to hooks and eyes; these would make a bold statement if used.
- **Velcro** An extremely versatile means of fastening two surfaces together; this comes in strips and dots, different widths and sizes. Available sticky-backed or ready to stitch.

With ever-increasing concern about environmental issues and sustainability, there is a growing consciousness of the need to be resourceful and inventive in our choice of, and our approach to, the materials we choose to work with.

A 'make do and mend' revival has encouraged us to take a more inspired and creative attitude towards 'upcycling' and re-purposing materials, which has led to a resurgence of bold and exploratory styles of contemporary appliqué.

The traditional rules of appliqué are being tested, stretched, pushed to their limits and, on occasions, well and truly broken. As a consequence, the boundaries and distinctions between appliqué and embellishment are becoming more and more blurred.

Above *Spots* wallhanging (Yana Krizka). An interactive wall hanging with detachable/interchangeable appliquéd spot motifs over covered buttons; soft-edged machine appliqué in cotton and felt onto a pieced cotton foundation (see page 125).

Below *Seams of Identity* number 1 (Julia Triston). From a series of work investigating the memories of cloth.

Appliqué or embellishment?

In our research for this book, we have considered the difference between appliqué and embellishment. For us, traditional appliqué is cloth on cloth, but has evolved to become much more decorative and experimental, and has started to encompass a world of 'anything goes' in terms of applying one 'material' to another 'material'. Appliqué still remains a shape, a motif, a slip (see Glossary, page 122), or something that you have made that is applied to a surface, which can be a starting or end point and further embellished.

An embellishment is traditionally a stitched-on 'item', such as a button, mirror, bead or sequin, which enriches and decorates a surface, often in a pattern.

Below *Neck Accessory* (Amy Fox). Lazer-cut motifs from the foundation fabric (leather) have been bonded back onto the surface with a heat press, so the positive and negative effect of the design can be seen; hand-made beads, sequins and leather trims further adorn the collar.

Above Triangle appliqué sample from Graduate Collection 2013 (Melissa McFadden). Hand-cut leather, suede and wool motifs hand stitched on to wool background.

Right *Future Deco* Graduate Collection 2013 (Melissa Edgar). Coloured and foiled leathers and cotton and glitter fabrics on foundations of polyester crepe and lycra. Hand-cut motifs are machine-stitched with one line, to allow movement within the fabric.

Conclusion to Part 4

Many artists are developing their own ways of working and defining their own practice by pushing the boundaries of the expected and traditional, so contemporary appliqué is continually evolving as a vibrant, cutting-edge art form. We hope our book inspires, motivates and empowers you and opens your eyes to the potential and scope of contemporary appliqué, both in terms of technique and materials.

As a maker, it is important to challenge yourself to venture beyond what you have considered to be the norm. By continuing to explore, develop, test and sample a wider range of tools, techniques and materials, your ideas, skills, understanding and confidence will grow and flourish and progress your own practice in exciting and unexpected ways.

Appliqué can embellish, adorn, enrich, decorate, enhance and beautify a surface. Enjoy playing and learning!

Glossary

abaca tissue Fabric tissue paper, easily torn, with a high 'wet strength'.

bodkin A big (round or flat) needle with a large eye. Used for threading tapes, cords and elastics through a stitched channel.

Bondaweb (Wonder Under) An iron-on fusible webbing with a non-stick paper backing.

cable stitch A free machine stitch used to create texture. A thick hand thread is wound around the bobbin and the machine tensions are altered. The surface to be stitched is placed right-side down under the needle and the bobbin thread is stitched onto, not through, the surface.

canvas Cotton fabric that is sturdy, heavy and tightly woven.

caparison An ornamental fabric covering spread over a horse's saddle or harness.

chenille needle A sharp, pointed needle with a large, long eye.

cuttlefish bone powder Ground up bone of a cuttlefish used in the 'prick and pounce' transfer method.

darning foot A spring-mounted sewing-machine foot used when free machine stitching.

embroidery needle A needle with a sharp point and a long eye.

fabric grain Woven fabrics are made from threads that run vertically (warp) and horizontally (weft) – when pulled along the warp or weft the fabric remains stable and does not stretch.

feather stitch A free machine embroidery stitch which creates loops of threads on the surface of the fabric, made by tightening the top tension and loosening the bottom tension.

feed dogs The 'toothed' bars beneath the presser foot that, when stitching, 'feed' the fabric underneath the needle.

fid A pointed tool used to push the fibres of a coarse fabric or rope apart to form a hole.

howdah A decorated canopied seat mounted on the back of an elephant.

kapok A silky, soft, downy fibre made from the seeds of the kapok tree, used for stuffing and padding.

Microtex needles A sewing-machine needle with a slim, sharp point for stitching through very fine or densely woven fabrics.

Kunin felt A soft non-frayable, easy-to-sew fabric ideal for burning and distressing techniques and padding.

motif A single shape or design that can be repeated to form a pattern.

netting needle A thin, slender shuttle used to make and repair fishing nets.

Opus Anglicanum Detailed and intricately worked embroidery created in Medieval England using gold, silver and silk threads on rich velvet or linen grounds.

pill/pilling The small balls of matted fibre that sometimes form when the surface of a piece of cloth is rubbed.

pin stitch A dainty embroidery stitch used along hems and edges on fine fabric, and to secure thin materials in appliqué work.

presser foot The sewing-machine foot that is used when stitching. These are available in many types.

scrim Very loosely woven, soft cotton fabric.

sharps General-sewing needles.

shisha mirror work Small pieces of glass, usually round, used as an embellishment in Indian embroidery.

silk carrier rods Tubes of compressed silk fibres.

slip A piece of embroidery or fabric that has been stitched, then applied to a new surface.

spiral punch A punch that mechanically twists and cuts out a circular hole when pressed into a suitable surface.

stiletto A pointed tool used to push holes in fabrics.

Suffolk puffs (yo-yos) These are made when a line of gathering stitches around the edge of a circle of fabric is drawn up so that the edges meet in the centre of the circle, creating a puffy form.

tailor's chalk A thin flat piece of hard chalk or soapstone traditionally used by tailors for making temporary marks on cloth.

tulle netting A fine, lightweight silk, rayon or nylon net, often starched and used for veils and ballet costumes.

Tyvek Strong, non-woven material that can be painted and stitched then distorted with a heat tool.

Velcro A fastener made of two strips of narrow fabric, one covered with flexible loops, the other with hooks; they stick to each other when pressed together and separate when pulled apart.

Vilene (interfacing) A non-woven material, it comes with, and without, iron-on glue on one side. Used to stabilize, add body to, strengthen fabrics and prevent stretching. Available in a variety of thicknesses to suit different weights of fabric.

voile A fine, lightweight fabric that is soft and sheer, usually in a cotton or cotton mix.

whip stitch A free machine embroidery stitch, created by lightening the top tension to bring the bottom thread through to the surface in 'spots'.

wireform A metal mesh that will hold its shape when manipulated; it can easily be moulded over a three-dimensional object such as a bowl and can be stitched into.

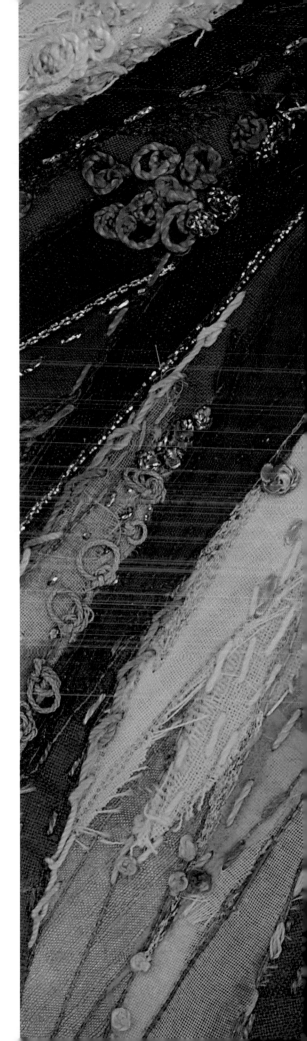

Right *Southern Oceans Plumage* (detail) (Rachel Lombard). Bonded cottons and abaca tissue with machine and hand stitch.

Suppliers

Art Van Go
The Studios
1 Stevenage Road
Knebworth
Hertfordshire
SG3 6AN
T: 01438 814946
www.artvango.co.uk
*Suppliers of fine art and
textile materials*

Barnyarns (Ripon) Ltd
Canal Wharf
Bondgate Green
Ripon
North Yorkshire
HG4 1AQ
T: 01765 690069
www.barnyarns.co.uk
*Machine embroidery threads,
needles and accessories*

Empress Mills
Empress Mills (1927) Ltd
Glyde Works
Byron Rd
Colne
Lancashire
BB8 0BQ
T: 01282 863181
www.empressmills.co.uk
*Fine sewing threads, haberdashery
and embroidery materials*

John James Needles
Entaco Limited
Unit 90
Washford Industrial Estate
Redditch
Worcestershire
B98 0EA
T: 01527 830941
www.jjneedles.com
*Sewing needles for embroidery
and specialist stitch work*

Kleins
11 D'Arblay Street
London
W1F 8DS
T: 020 7437 6162
www.kleins.co.uk
Appliqué and haberdashery suppliers

MacCulloch & Wallis
25-26 Dering Street
London
W1S 1AT
T: 020 7629 0311
www.macculloch-wallis.co.uk
*Haberdashery, millinery and
corsetry supplies*

Oliver Twists
22 Phoenix Road
Crowther
Washington
Tyne & Wear
NE38 0AD
T: 0191 4166016
www.etsy.com/uk/shop/OliverTwists
Fibres.
*Hand-dyed hand and machine
embroidery threads, fibres, felts
and fabrics*

Below *Spot* motifs (Yana Krizka). Layered
appliqué cotton 'spots' which are detachable
from the hanging and interchangeable with
each other; soft-edged machine appliqué in
cotton onto felt base (see page 119).

Simply Solids
3 Orchard Street West
Longwood
Huddersfield
HD3 4TE
T: 07545 153039
www.simplysolids.co.uk
100% cotton fabrics

Texere Yarns Ltd
College Mill
Barkerend Road
Bradford
West Yorkshire
BD1 4AU
T: 01274 722191
www.texere-yarns.co.uk
*Dyed and undyed threads and yarns
suitable for hand embroidery*

V V Rouleaux
102 Marylebone Lane
London
W1U 2AD
T: 020 7224 5179
www.vvrouleaux.com
Ribbons, trimmings and braids

Whaleys (Bradford) Ltd
Harris Court
Great Horton
Bradford
West Yorkshire
BD7 4EQ
T: 01274 576718
www.whaleys-bradford.ltd.uk
*Fabrics and interfacings – many
suitable for dyeing*

Julia Triston
T: 07855 219253
www.juliatriston.com
*Workshops, day schools, residencies
and courses in contemporary art,
design, stitch and world textiles*

Rachel Lombard
T: 07986 852587
www.rachellombardtextileart.
talktalk.net
*Contemporary stitched textile art and
design, workshops and illustrated
talks; based in County Durham*

STITCHBUSINESS
www.stitchbusiness.com
*Independent, international stitch
school offering creative courses and
masterclasses in design and art
textiles, in Durham City or by
distance learning*

Below Beaver badges 2013 (Seb Miller).
Beaver uniform with appliquéd
achievement badges.

Bibliography and further reading

Bawden, Juliet, *Appliqué Style*, Cassell, 1997

Bawden, Juliet, *The Art and Craft of Appliqué*, Mitchell Beazley Publishing, 1991

Beal, Margaret, *Fusing Fabrics*, B T Batsford, Ltd, 2005

Brooks, Stephen and McIlwain, John (eds), *The Overlord Embroidery*, Portsmouth City Council, 1999

Brown, Pauline, *Appliqué*, Merehurst Limited, 1989

Cohen, David and Anderson, Scott, *A Visual Language*, Herbert Press, 2006

Dean, Beryl, *Creative Appliqué*, Studio Vista Ltd, 1970

Gillow, John, *African Textiles*, Thames & Hudson, 2003

Gillow, John and Sentence, Bryan, *World Textiles*, Thames & Hudson, 1999

Greenlees, Kay, *Creating Sketchbooks for Embroiderers and Textile Artists*, Batsford, 2005

Harvey, Janet, *The Traditional Textiles of Central Asia*, Thames & Hudson, 1996

Holmes, Cas, *The Found Object in Textile Art*, Batsford 2010

Holmes, Val, *The Encyclopedia of Machine Embroidery*, Batsford, 2003

Howard, Constance, *Inspiration for Embroidery*, Batsford, 1967

Mathews, Kate, *Molas!*, Lark Books, 2000

Meech, Sandra, *Connecting Art to Stitch*, Batsford, 2009

Meech, Sandra, *Contemporary Quilts: Design, Surface and Stitch*, Batsford, 2003

Paine, Sheila, *Embroidery from India and Pakistan*, British Museum Press, 2001

Pipes, Alan, *Foundations of Art and Design*, Laurence King Publishing 2003

Singer, Margo & Spyrou, Mary, *Textile Arts Multicultural Traditions*, A&C Black, 2003

Staniland, Kay, *Medieval Craftsmen Embroiderers*, British Museum Press, 1997

Synge, Lanto (general ed), *The Royal School of Needlework Book of Needlework and Embroidery*, Wm Collins Sons & Co Ltd, 1986

Thittichai, Kim, *Hot Textiles*, Batsford, 2007

Thomas, Mary and Eaton, Jan, *Mary Thomas's Dictionary of Embroidery Stitches*, Hodder & Stoughton, 1998

Triston, Julia and Lombard, Rachel, *How to be Creative in Textile Art*, Batsford, 2011

Wong, Wucius, *The Principles of Form and Design*, John Wiley & Sons Inc, 1993

Acknowledgements

Julia and Rachel would like to thank Steven Landles for his stunning photography and patience, and Joan Baker for her constructive editing, comments and helpful suggestions.

We would both like to extend our appreciation and thanks to: STITCHBUSINESS students, fellow members of Fusion and members of Prism, The 62 Group and the Textile Study Group, along with many other talented practitioners, new designers and artists who have generously submitted their inspiring appliqué work.

We are grateful to Annette Collinge at the Embroiderers' Guild for the loan of precious historical textiles, and other keepers and curators of treasured appliqué textiles – in particular Durham Cathedral, The Bowes Museum (Barnard Castle), The Quilt Museum and Gallery (York) and The Oriental Museum (Durham University). Thanks also go to Anthea Godfrey for advice, guidance and counsel and the family of Rebecca Crompton.

This book is much richer and more exciting for your contributions; thanks to you all for pushing the conventional boundaries, being passionate about stitch and keeping the art of appliqué alive.

Picture credits

All images by Steven Landles Photography, except for: pages 1 and 94 (left) Mandy Pattullo; page 4 Neil Cooper; page 7 Emily Notman, page 11 Photograph © The State Hermitage Museum /photo by Vladimir Terebenin, Leonard Kheifets, Yuri Molodkovets; page 12 The Bowes Museum, Barnard Castle, UK; page 13 R. Haddon; page 14 Photography by Art Van Go; page 15 The Quilters' Guild of the British Isles; page 16 (left) Victoria & Albert Museum, London, UK / The Bridgeman Art Library; page 17 D-Day Museum, Portsmouth; page 18 Julie Bull; page 19 Laura McCafferty; page 23 The Oriental Museum, Durham University, Durham City, UK / Kate Weightman; page 25 Ben Smith Images; page 26, 73 Tilleke Schwarz; page 28 Michael Wicks; page 30 (left) Lisa Stirling; page 33 Janet Browne; page 36 Lesli Michaelis Onusk; page 37 Ruth Issett; page 40 Joanne Edwards; page 43 Sussie Alhburg; page 47 Debbie Lyddon; page 79 (left) Bill Bradshaw Photography; page 80, David Ramkalawon; page 81 (main image) Sara Leigh Lewis; page 87, 88, 89 (drawings), 95, 112 Julia Triston; page 92, 93 (left) Rhiannon Williams; 93 (top),115 Samantha Scott; page 94 (top) Beverley Holmes-Wright; page 98 (top) Alison Stewart; page 102, 103 (left) Karen Suzuki; page 103 (top) Joanne Edwards; page 105 Matthew Aland; page 106 Eva Logan Photography; page 107, 114 Jamie McGarvey; page 109 Emily Notman; page 113 Kathryn Cullen; page 118 Sophie O'Brien; page 120 Amy Fox; page 121 (left) Melissa McFadden; page 121 (right) Melissa Edgar; page 123 Rachel Lombard.

Below and opposite
Roundels, Meo Tribe costume fragments (collection of Julia Triston).

Index